B-1 LANCER

in detail & scale

Wayne Wachsmuth

TAB BOOKS
Blue Ridge Summit, PA

Airlife Publishing Ltd.
England

CONTRIBUTORS AND SOURCES:

SSGT Steve Bailey, USAF	Jim Galloway	TSGT Butch Molnar, USAF	Baldur Sveinsson
Dana Bell	Bob Greby	Warren Munkasy	Kathy Wachsmuth
COL Knox Bishop, USAF	Geof Hayes	CPT Gail Reiner, USAF	John Wahl
MAJ Denny Blodgett, USAF	Ed Hjort	Erik Simonsen	Steve Zaloga
CMSGT Tom Brewer, USAF (Ret.)	CPT Kevin Krueger, USAF	Tom Starnes	U.S. Air Force
MAJ Paul Cusac, USAF	Don Logan	Ed Sveum	U.S. Air Force Museum
SSGT Greg Dudley, USAF	R. McNeil	CPT Bill Shockley, USAF	Rockwell International

Edited by Bert Kinzey

Many photographs in this publication are credited to their contributors. Photographs with no credit indicated were taken by the author. Where known, the DAVA (Defense Audio Visual Agency) ID number is listed for DOD photographs.

FIRST EDITION
FIRST PRINTING

Published in United States by

TAB BOOKS
Blue Ridge Summit, PA 17294-0214

Library of Congress Cataloging
in Publication Data:

Wachsmuth, Wayne.
B-1 bomber / by Wayne Wachsmuth.
ISBN 0-8306-5050-4 (pbk.)
1. B-1 bomber. I. Title.
UG1242.B6W33   1990
358.4′2—dc20   90-11038
                                      CIP

First published in Great Britain in 1990
by Airlife Publishing Ltd.
7 St. John's Hill, Shrewsbury, SY1 1JE

British Library Cataloging in
Publication Data
Wachsmuth, Wayne
B - 1 bomber.
1. Bomber aeroplanes
I. Title   II. Series
623.7463

ISBN 1-85310-622-4

TAB BOOKS offers software for
sale. For information and a catalog,
please contact TAB Software Department,
Blue Ridge Summit, PA 17294-0850

Questions regarding the content of this book
should be addressed to:

Reader Inquiry Branch
TAB BOOKS
Blue Ridge Summit, PA 17294-0214

Front cover: Although the B-1 is one of the most powerful aircraft in the world today, its sleek blended lines make it a thing of beauty in flight. Many people forget that the main reason such destructive weapon systems are built is to insure that they never be used. This is the irony of strategic weapons that are designed not only to defend America, but to protect peace. If the B-1Bs accomplish their primary mission, that of strategic deterrence, their awesome capabilities will never have to be used in anger. (USAF DF-ST-88-07178)

Rear cover: This in-flight photograph of the instrument panel reveals the thermometer type displays for the engine instruments and the Vertical Situation Display (VSD) screens. Note that they indicate that the aircraft is in a left bank. (USAF DF-ST-88-03482)

INTRODUCTION

B-1A number four is the subject of this head-on photograph. Notice the extensive amount of ground support equipment and the lowered leading edge slats on the wing. The inner portion of the raised spoilers can be seen on each side of the photograph. On B-1As the spoilers were usually in the raised position when the aircraft was on the ground and the power was turned off. The only exception to this was when the hydraulics were intentionally bled off to lower the spoilers for publicity photographs. This photograph was taken while the aircraft was painted in the desert camouflage scheme. (Simonsen via Munkasy)

Over the years, the B-1 bomber has received much publicity. From the beginning, its critics have screamed loud and long about deficiencies and shortcomings that the aircraft was supposed to have. Like any other sophisticated system, the B-1 has had some problems, but most of what the critics have had to say was more noise than fact, and clearly illustrated that they were uninformed at the very least. In most cases they simply did not know what they were talking about, nor did they have the expertise to fully understand the problem or its solutions. For example, an editorial in a newspaper in Norfolk, Virginia, blasted the B-1 for its alleged deficiencies. It was obvious that the writer of that column had absolutely no understanding of the B-1 system, and it is doubtful that he had even seen one of the aircraft, much less studied it and its development in any detail. This sort of irresponsible journalism misleads the American public, who often take what these writers say as being factual information. Readers all too often believe that, simply because someone gets what he or she has written printed in a newspaper, it automatically makes that person an expert. They do not realize that they are reading something that was written by an uninformed and unqualified source.

But irresponsible journalists have not been the only ones to use misinformation to fight against the B-1 and other programs. A number of senators, congressmen, and at least one congresswoman were involved with the anti-B-1 movement from the start. They claimed that the B-1 program was an effort to keep North American's (now Rockwell) production lines continually producing bombers. The fact was, except for a few B-45 Tornado medium bombers that were built in the 1950s, North American has not put any bomber design into production for the U.S. Air Force since the B-25 that served in World War II. Designed prior to the war in the 1930s, the B-25 was most famous for being the aircraft used in the Doolittle raid on Japan in April 1942. It later served in all theaters of the war, and was retired from combat duties shortly thereafter. Since then, with the exception of the few B-45 medium bombers, North American, and most other American aircraft manufacturers, had been out of the business of building long range strategic bombers. North American did design and build two prototypes of the XB-70, but this program was cancelled before the bomber was put into production. This hardly constitutes the "continual stream" of strategic bombers coming off the production lines that these elected officials complained about. The last B-52 had been delivered in 1962, and was the only strategic bomber with intercontinental range in

Low level penetration and weapons delivery are necessary for survival in today's sophisticated high threat environment. Here a B-1 delivers a practice weapon while a T-38 chase plane records the action. (Rockwell via Munkasy)

service. The few B-58s and only seventy-six FB-111As were the only other strategic bombers built in the interim, and both of these aircraft were medium bombers that lacked both the payload and range requirements of an intercontinental bomber.

These are the facts about America's bomber force and its production at the time the anti-B-1 movement tried to prevent the Air Force from developing a much needed replacement for the B-52. But these elected officials and their supporters lied to the American public about the B-1 in an effort to have it cancelled. They even showed a picture that they claimed to be B-1s rolling off the assembly line. However, this photograph was taken before even the first B-1 prototype was built! In actuality, the aircraft in the photo were F-111s, which had little more in common with the B-1 than the fact that both aircraft had variable-sweep wings. But these people were able to convince President Carter to cancel the B-1 when there was no alternative to replace the aging fleet of B-52s. When Carter cancelled the B-1, the newest B-52 was almost twenty years old, and the average age of the fleet was much older. However, the interceptors and missile systems in the Soviet Union and the Warsaw Pact that were designed to defend against them were considerably newer. Almost all B-52s had passed the quarter-century mark in operational service when the first B-1 finally became operational. At the same time, the Carter Administration agreed to count retired and unflyable B-52s in the "boneyard" at Davis-Monthan Air Force Base, and even hulks of former B-52s mounted on pedestals near the gates at Air Force Bases, as part of America's bomber force for the purposes of the SALT treaty! At least as far as numbers went, this made the U.S. bomber force appear much larger than it actually was. All Carter's cancellation did was to delay the B-1 in becoming operational by disrupting the program, and it drove up the costs for the aircraft and its development. Although President Carter's many ill-advised decisions with respect to the military did the most damage to the Navy, it was his decision to cancel the B-1 that is considered by many to be his biggest blunder. Fortunately, it was corrected by President Reagan in time to restore credibility to the only recallable leg of America's triad of strategic deterrence.

Considering the complexity of the B-1 program, and the political dickering with its development, the actual hardware has had relatively few problems, and most of these were corrected. In one case, there was a perceived problem when no actual problem existed at all. The Defensive Avionics System was originally asked to do far more than the available technology could provide. Even today's state-of-the-art avionics have not advanced far enough to attain the capability that the Air Force originally had hoped the system would have. When technology could not meet the unrealistic goal, the B-1 program was criticized. This makes about as much sense as criticizing aircraft manufacturers during World War II for not building supersonic aircraft! The technology simply was not available at the time to do so.

Other problems surfaced during flight testing. This testing was interrupted by Carter's cancellation of the program, and this made matters worse. But every deficiency discovered during flight testing was jumped on by the critics as proof that the B-1 should not be built. Little did it matter that these problems were subsequently corrected. After all, the reason you do flight testing in the first place is to discover such problems and come up with fixes. But the doomsayers would have you think that no problems should be found in testing. Systems far simpler than a complex combat aircraft need extensive evaluation, and the fact is that relatively few problems were discovered by the B-1 flight test program. Those that were found have been fixed, and in most cases now exceed requirements.

By comparison, the capabilities of the B-1 system and its successes have been considerable. Of course, the same people that are so quick to amplify and distort any shortcomings that they don't even understand, will never write about the remarkable accomplishments of the same system they criticize.

This book is written by Wayne Wachsmuth, a former bomber pilot with the Strategic Air Command who has time in the B-47, the B-52, and the FB-111A bombers. He has flown the B-52 in combat. Recently retired from the Air Force, Wayne visited the B-1 crews at McConnell

Here a B-1A refuels from a KC-10 tanker high over the desert. It is obvious that the Strategic Scheme was not designed for this environment. (Rockwell via Munkasy)

AFB, and talked to them extensively. He personally knew and worked with some of the original B-1 flight test crews while he was still in the Air Force. He talked with other people who had been with the program from day one. In the final analysis, it is the crews that have to put their lives on the line flying an aircraft in combat who can best tell you the worth of the system. They will be the first to praise it if it is good, and the first to complain if it isn't. It is the people who have to operate the aircraft day in and day out who have the best understanding and who are best qualified to judge its merits--not some uninformed journalist who has never even seen the aircraft.

Wayne has written the narrative of this book with the understanding that comes from once having been "in the trenches" as a bomber pilot. His personal knowledge, that is derived from his own experience, helps the reader gain an understanding of the B-1 from a SAC bomber pilot's point of view. Wayne addresses the criticisms that have been leveled at the B-1 and presents the facts. Although the size and scope of this book does not permit an in-depth look at these criticisms, he covers each of them with enough information and explanation to show what the truth really is. He also discusses each of the four crashes that have occurred since the first B-1 took to the air, and presents the facts that show that none of these were the fault of the aircraft or its design.

As is the case with all of the books in the Detail & Scale Series, the primary purpose of this publication is to show the subject in detail. To do this, Wayne spent a lot of time on the ramp with the B-1, taking scores of photographs to show its many details. Differences between the B-1A and B-1B are clearly explained and illustrated. Details of the interior, landing gear, engines, weapons bays, armament, defensive systems, electronics, vents and intakes, and much more are covered with extensive photographs that were taken by Wayne specifically for this publication. Official drawings supplement the photographic coverage. Wayne personally drew the scale drawings that illustrate both the B-1A and B-1B. These are the best and most up-to-date ever published on the B-1. Wayne included additional scale drawings that show the complete camouflage schemes used on the B-1A and B-1B. Federal Standard numbers are provided for the colors in the camouflage patterns. These drawings, along with a section in the narrative about the B-1's paint schemes and markings, make this publication the first to correctly and completely identify the various colors, schemes, and patterns used on the prototypes and production aircraft.

For scale modelers, we have included our usual modeler's section at the end of the book. Wayne is an avid modeler, and has served as head judge for many years at the IPMS/USA national contests. This, along with his in-depth knowledge of the B-1, makes him the most qualified person anywhere to review the scale model kits of the B-1 that are presently available. His complete modelers section will be most helpful to scale modelers, because it tells what is right and wrong with each kit, and which are the best kits to use. A decal summary is also provided.

Both Wayne and Detail & Scale hope that this publication will help the reader understand the B-1 bomber, its development, capabilities, and its production based on the facts, not on the hearsay of uninformed and unqualified journalists or the politicians. We hope that the scores of detailed photographs and drawings, illustrating the many systems and components of this complex aircraft, will provide a basic understanding of how all of the parts work together to form an effective weapon system.

Bert Kinzey
Detail & Scale

DEVELOPMENTAL HISTORY

When President Reagan reinstated the B-1 program, an IOC of 1986 was specified for the aircraft. That date was met, and the B-1B now provides an all-important part of America's strategic triad of nuclear deterrence for peace. This photograph shows the positions of the wings, stabilators, and other control surfaces on the B-1B when the aircraft is on the ground. Note that on the B-1B, the spoilers are down in this "at rest" configuration, rather than being up as they were on the B-1As. Details of the overwing fairing are also visible. *(Simonsen via Munkasy)*

BACKGROUND AND DEVELOPMENT

When the first B-1B went on alert in October of 1986 and reached the goal of Initial Operational Capability (IOC) on schedule, it passed just one more milestone in what has to be one of the most protracted weapon system development sagas ever recorded. To go back to the origins of the system, we must look all the way back to the last years of B-52 procurement, since the requirement to find a replacement for the Stratofortress has been the driving force behind the many studies and aborted programs witnessed since the last B-52H rolled off the line in 1962. Since then, there has been a complete change in the tactics needed to penetrate hostile airspace and survive. Speaking as a B-47, B-52, and FB-111A pilot, the survival part has always been right at the top of my list, and the evolution of tactics has been fascinating to watch. The B-58 Hustler became operational in 1960, but as a medium bomber, it did not have the legs or the payload of the B-52. After only ten years of duty, it was phased out because of several problems. The worst were fatigue and the inability to terrain follow in dirty weather or at night.

The XB-70 program was plagued by two major problems, cost and survivability. Cost was an inherent factor in pushing the current state-of-the-art, and survivability problems were brought on by anti-aircraft systems employing post-launch guidance, ie. surface-to-air missiles. When Gary Powers' U-2 was shot down in May 1960, the handwriting was on the wall for the high altitude penetrator. While the high altitude environment did not become impenetrable overnight, it made no sense to develop more bombers that had to go in at high altitude.

About the same time, the fight over whether or not the manned bomber was really a necessary part of America's strategic force was being fought over and over again. To those of us in the business, it seemed like this battle was fought thirty or forty times! However often that debate has raged, the answer has always been that the inherent advantages of manned aircraft make them worth the effort and expense of keeping them in the inventory. That was the conclusion in 1960, although the configuration of the next generation of bombers was still in doubt.

In the early to mid-1960s, there were several studies that consumed a large quantity of the alphabet for acronyms: SLAP (Subsonic Low Altitude Penetrator), ERSA (Extended Range Strategic Aircraft), AMP (Advanced Manned Penetrator), LAMP (Low Altitude Manned Penetrator), AMPSS (Advanced Manned Precision Strike System), and AMSA (Advanced Manned Strategic Aircraft). But when all of the dust settled, the letters still spelled MANNED BOMBER. The final study (AMSA) would lead to the release of the Request For Proposal (RFP) to the aviation industry in late 1969.

Barely a month before the release of the RFP, the Strategic Air Command had taken possession of its initial FB-111A, the first of a fleet of only seventy-six aircraft. Originally proposed to be a force of 210 aircraft, the number had been driven downward by the politicians until the reduced number guaranteed that the program would be nearly as expensive to build and maintain as the original number of 210. The FB-111A was an excellent penetrator, and a great deal was learned with it concerning the ultra low level environment and state-of-the-art avionics. However, the small fleet still came off a distant second to the venerable B-52 when it came to range and payload capabilities.

The RFP, that was released in November of 1969, spelled out several characteristics the new aircraft was to possess. Among the more important were an escape module, nuclear hardness, central integrated test system (CITS), and low altitude ride control. The escape module requirement was based on the F/FB-111 experience, and while I always had an equal number of takeoffs and landings in the F/FB-111, the module was a definite plus. There are crewmembers walking around today that owe their survival to the escape module. Nuclear hardness was used with one of the buzz phrases circulating in that time frame--electro magnetic pulse or EMP. The idea was to keep from frying all of your avionics when the base you just launched from was hit. Any time you were in the proximity of a nuclear detonation during the mission (including from your own weapons) there was an electromagnetic pulse generated by the detonation that could destroy electronic gear and render the systems in a combat aircraft absolutely useless. The CITS meant that if you dispersed the aircraft in times of tension to reduce vulnerability, all of the test equipment that the Avionics Maintenance Squadron owned did not have to go with

you. Yet a capability to properly maintain the avionics still existed.

The low altitude ride control requirement was probably the most important from the average crew dog's point of view, since any aircraft that flies close to the ground at high speed is affected by turbulence. A large aircraft with the crew stations some distance from the center of lift is the worst possible case. The early B-52s were an excellent case in point with the aft gunner's station. I have seen gunners whose helmets were cracked and broken from hitting the sides of the compartment during low level flight where the speed did not even exceed 300 knots.

While the Air Force had been studying the future bomber, the major manufacturers had been conducting their own inquiries, and three of them were ready when the RFP was released. General Dynamics, who had built the B-36, B-58, and FB-111A, Boeing, who had produced the B-47 and B-52, and Rockwell (North American), the prime contractor for the XB-70, all had proposals. A little over six months after the RFP was released, the Air Force announced that Rockwell had been chosen to build the test airframes and conduct the research, development, test, and evaluation (RDT&E).

The original contract called for five flying and two structural test airframes along with forty of General Electric's F101 engines that had been chosen to power the new bomber. Rockwell lost no time starting on the airframe mockup that would be used for design approval. In addition to giving the Air Force something to look at to evaluate the design, the mockup let the engineers check things like space for equipment, where the cable runs had to go, the length and shape of tubing runs, and other items that are now done by a computer as it was for the B-2.

While the mockup was being built and evaluated, the political turbulence that had dogged the program from its earliest days continued. This resulted in a reduction in the test program to three flying and one structural test airframe and only twenty-seven engines. Additionally, the production schedule was stretched, meaning that the

One of the B-1As is shown here under construction at Palmdale.   (Rockwell via Munkasy)

This is the mockup that was constructed for design verification. The right side was built in cutaway so that the interior structure was exposed. This was done to enable engineers to check equipment fit and the locations of the runs for wiring and tubing.
(USAF SDAN 182657)

The cockpit in the mockup shows few differences with that in the final production aircraft. Note the large circular moving map display just to the left of center, and the fact that the B-1 is equipped with fighter type control columns rather than the usual yokes found on most bombers and other large aircraft.

(USAF SDAN 182653)

first airframe would have to carry the flight test load alone for over a year. The danger existed that any accident involving this airframe would bring the program to a halt. Further slips and stretches plagued the program, and its 3000 suppliers and subcontractors caused scheduling problems that in turn caused price increases and new stretches or changes to try to reduce costs. The result was that the program no longer was an effort to build a cost effective weapon, but to build a weapon to fit a cost ceiling. While all the political pulling and tugging was going on with the checkbook, Rockwell continued with airframe number one in fits and starts as the changes kept coming in. Finally, on October 26, 1974, 74-0158 was ceremoniously rolled out at Palmdale, and on December 23rd, it made its first flight.

The test program proceeded with more than the usual amount of caution, because there was only one aircraft. It was with much relief that number three, 74-0160, was integrated into the test program in January 1976. The second airframe, 74-0159, was used as the structural test airframe, and following its refurbishing for flight, it too entered the flight test arena in May of 1976.

While the flight testing progressed, other facets of the program had turned up the usual problems, the most serious having to do with the crew module. Sled testing had shown the module to be unstable at speeds over 350 knots, and since any attempt to fix it (assuming it could be fixed) would need massive infusions of money, the decision was made to equip all airframes after the third with ejection seats.

While the airspeed and altitude envelope was being expanded by continuous flight testing, the fourth airframe was authorized, and production started on it in August 1975. Several visible changes were made to it, and these included the elimination of the escape module with its large stabilizing vanes, revision of the engine nacelles, and a slightly different configuration for the nose gear linkage.

All of this was proceeding apace in Southern California, but nothing had changed on the political scene. The tug of war still raged between the supporters and opponents of the program, with probably the most decisive event being the election of Jimmy Carter to the Presidency in the fall of 1976. In the spring of 1977 it became

The first three B-1As are seen here together on the ramp at Edwards AFB. Number two is in the foreground, and numbers one (left) and three (right) are in the background. (USAF)

known that the price per copy of the B-1 would exceed 100 million dollars, and even the cheering section swallowed hard. After some preliminary maneuvering, the President announced on June 30th that B-1 procurement would be cancelled. The number four airframe was to be completed, and money would be expended for continued testing, but the fleet of production aircraft would not be bought. Supposedly, the deterrent capability would be maintained by the newly emerging cruise missile. To keep at least one iron in the fire, Rockwell proposed to the Air Force several R&D programs, and the Air Force then went to the Secretary of Defense with a new bucket of acronyms. These included NTP (Near Term Penetrator),

SWL (Strategic Weapons Launcher), CMCA (Cruise Missile Carrier Aircraft), MRB (Multi-Role Bomber), and LRCA (Long Range Combat Aircraft). The upshot was a test program called BPE (Bomber Penetration Evaluation) to be funded until January 1981. Its emphasis was on flying the B-1 test aircraft against simulated threats in Red Flag type environments to see what the odds really were of getting in and, equally important, getting back out of the target area.

In February 1979, number four, 76-0174, was added to the fleet, and for the first time, a complete aircraft with a full avionics suite was available for testing. When BPE was finished in the spring of 1981, several options were

The third B-1A, 74-0160, was actually the second to fly, because the second aircraft was used first as a structural test airframe. Here B-1A number three poses for the camera and provides a look at its underside details and markings. (Rockwell via Munkasy)

B-1A number four takes off on its first flight. Note the large dielectric panels on the glove area of the wing. This aircraft was the first to be equipped with ejection seats, because the crew escape module used on the first three prototypes was found to be unsatisfactory. *(Rockwell via Munkasy)*

on the table as far as the future of the manned bomber was concerned. First, the avionics in the B-52 could be refurbished. Second, the FB-111A airframe could be stretched to extend range and expand its capabilities. The third option was to use a commercial jumbo jet as a cruise missile carrier, and the fourth possibility was to build an advanced copy of the B-1. Given those choices, the B-1 option was clearly the best bet, and in October 1981, President Reagan announced that 100 B-1s would be bought with an IOC in 1986. The cost of the entire fleet was to be under 20.5 billion dollars. These restrictions were to cause problems with the program's development,

but the Air Force believed that without them the program would not sell.

By this time, the four existing airframes had been designated B-1As, and the first step was to take the two with the least time on them, numbers two and four, and bring them up to B-1B standards. This would provide a head start on the flight testing. Number two, 74-0159, started test flights in March 1983, and was joined by number four, 76-0174, in July that same year. Less than a month later, number two was destroyed in a crash during a test flight. An aft center of gravity condition was inadvertently allowed to develop, and the aircraft pitched up

This is one of the rare photographs that shows B-1A number four with the EVS deployed. It is just aft of the nose gear, and the small black rectangle is the sensor window. *(USAF)*

and became uncontrollable. The aircraft was still equipped with the module, and ejection was initiated by the crew. During the descent, the parachute bridle did not reposition to allow the module to land level, and the subsequent impact on the forward end caused fatal injuries to the Rockwell test pilot and lesser injuries to the other crew members.

The following month, B-1B number one, 82-0001, was rolled out of the Palmdale plant and started flight testing on October 18th. This was fortunate, since the testing lost little or no headway from the loss of B-1A number two. The program continued to proceed with the steadily increasing flow of aircraft from the production line at Palmdale until the first operational B-1B was turned over to SAC at Dyess AFB, Texas, on June 29, 1985. It was thirty years to the day since the first B-52 was delivered to the Air Force. However, this event was marred by the fact that B-1B number two, the aircraft chosen to be the first to be delivered, suffered foreign object damage to an engine when it landed at Offutt AFB enroute to Dyess. Therefore, B-1B number one had to be substituted at the last minute.

Normal teething problems were experienced as the fleet became operational, with the fuel leakage problem getting the most press time until teams were sent from the Air Force logistics depots to teach the contractor how to do the job properly. Meanwhile, deliveries continued to the 96th Bomb Wing at Dyess, followed by the 28th BW at Ellsworth, the 319th BW at Grand Forks, and lastly, the 384th BW at McConnell AFB. The one-hundredth and last B-1B was received by the 384th BW in April 1988.

PRESENT DISPOSITION

Today, three of the four B-1As still exist. Number one is at an ECM test site at Griffiss AFB, New York, number three is used as a weapons upload trainer at Lowry AFB, Colorado, and number four is at the Air Force Museum at Wright Patterson AFB, Ohio. Number two was destroyed in the aft CG accident at Edwards AFB, California.

The four operational wings of B-1Bs include the 96th Bomb Wing at Dyess AFB, Texas. The 96th BW has one bomb squadron and a crew training squadron. Twenty-nine B-1Bs are assigned to this wing. The 28th Bomb Wing is stationed at Ellsworth AFB, South Dakota, and has two bomb squadrons. The 28th BW has a usual complement of thirty-five B-1Bs. The 319th Bomb Wing is based at Grand Forks AFB, North Dakota, and has one bomb squadron. Seventeen B-1Bs are assigned to this wing. The 384th Bomb Wing at McConnell AFB, Kansas, also has one bomb squadron with seventeen B-1Bs. Two B-1Bs are assigned to Edwards AFB, California, for test purposes.

THE AIRCRAFT AND ITS DESIGN

The B-1A and B-1B share airframes that are heavily blended in the wing-fuselage area. They have variable-sweep wings, and an empennage of conventional layout. Readily observable differences include the shapes of the forward and aft radomes and a longer forward avionics bay on the B-1B. The B-1As with the escape module have large stabilization vanes aft of the cockpit, and the engine intake lips are simplified and raked aft on the -B. The overwing fairing is more complex and has inflatable seals on the -B. There are several large blade antennas on the top and bottom of the B-1B, and there are small windows at the OSO and DSO stations on the -B.

The structure is conventional with aluminum alloy being used predominately, and titanium being used in the heavy load-bearing areas like the wing carry-through structure. The General Electric F101 engines are under-

Still in a zinc chromate finish, the one-hundredth and last B-1B is rolled out of the Palmdale plant. In the background, the twenty-sixth B-1B and an F-106 chase plane fly past the ceremony.
(Simonsen)

This excellent photograph shows a B-1B on the ground with its support equipment around it. Markings for the refueling door are clearly visible.
(Rockwell via Munkasy)

slung in nacelles with an auxiliary power unit (APU) being located in each nacelle. Flight control surfaces are conventional, with roll control being provided by wing spoilers and asymmetric horizontal stab deflection. Conventional rudder and elevator surfaces are used for yaw and pitch control. Two small vanes on each fuselage side above the nose gear are part of the structural mode control System (SMCS) that dampens oscillations caused by turbulence and helps prevent airframe and crew fatigue. The primary crewmembers, pilot, co-pilot, offensive systems operator, and defensive systems operator, are supplied with ejection seats, while the two instructor positions must exit the aircraft through the entry hatch in any emergency that requires a bailout.

Offensive avionics include the Avionics Control Unit Complex (ACUC), a single Inertial Navigation System (INS), a Doppler Velocity Sensor (DVS), the Offensive Radar Set (ORS), two radar altimeters, and the Terrain Following Avionics Control Unit (TFACU). The offensive capabilities are proving to be very accurate, and the radar has shown it is capable of picking out individual posts in a chain link fence. In the 1989 SAC bombing and navigation competition (Proud Shield), the 28th Bomb Wing with its B-1Bs and KC-135s took the Fairchild Trophy for the overall best bombing and navigation scores. This was the earliest that any new weapons system has won the competition in terms of operational years going into the exercise. Of course the critics and the journalists never published anything like this about the aircraft.

The defensive avionics systems includes the AN/ALQ-168A Radio Frequency Surveillance/Electronic Countermeasure System (RFS/ECMS), the Tail Warning Function (TWF), the AN/ASQ-184 offensive avionics system Defensive Management System (DMS), and the Expendable Countermeasures (EXCM) system.

Aircraft systems are controlled by the Electrical Multiplex (EMUX) system that is essentially a redundant computer that can use the same wiring to pass commands to each aircraft system, thus saving weight by reducing the amount of wire needed. The EMUX system also controls and manages the electrical loads, and interfaces with the Central Integrated Test System (CITS). CITS is a system that continuously monitors all aircraft systems, and it displays any malfunctions to the crew on the CITS control and display (CCD) panel. It also records the data for maintenance use after a flight. It has been said that the B-1 is a "large computer system surrounded by fuel and engines," and it seems that this is not very wide of the mark.

CONTROVERSY

Like a great many other modern weapon systems, the B-1 has come in for nearly as much "friendly fire" as it would get from the "hostiles" if it is ever used in anger. Some is warranted, most is not, and the waters are muddied extensively by politics. This leaves the casual observer to wonder where the truth lies. The best way to approach the problem is to take the various claims one at a time, remove the hype, and see what that leaves.

To date one B-1A and three B-1Bs have been destroyed in accidents for a rate per 100,000 hours of flying time that is still better than that of the B-52 at the same period in its operational life. Specifically, the B-1A was lost because the crew had the wings swept aft, and the fuel shifted aft for a test. The crew then swept the wings forward and forgot to move the fuel. They missed a caution light that advised of the problem. When they reduced speed for the next test, the aircraft pitched up and stalled.

The first B-1B was lost to a bird strike, and much has been made over the fact that a BIRD can knock down the B-1. The normal cruise speed at low level is just under 1000 feet per second, and the bird that was struck was a pelican weighing between twelve and fifteen pounds. This produced an impact greater than if a twelve pound Napoleon canon of Civil War vintage was fired point blank into the aircraft! Fuel and hydraulic lines were severed, and the resulting fire caused the loss of the aircraft. Kelvar panels have been added to protect critical areas, but if a bird of significant size is hit, damage will be severe. That is just one of the hazards of low level flight, and any aircraft, not just the B-1, can be brought down by striking a bird of significant size in the wrong place.

The next two -Bs were lost in rapid succession in November of 1988. The first of these two losses was due to material failure of a fuel fitting over the engine nacelle. When the fitting failed, it caused an in-flight fire, and the crew was forced to eject. The other B-1B was lost when it was allowed to descend too far on an instrument approach, and it hit poles at an altitude of thirty feet above the ground and slightly over one-half mile from the end of the runway. Regardless of whether the crew was flying a B-1 or any other type of aircraft, the result would have been the same under the circumstances. It can be seen that none of the losses can be attributed to a design problem with the aircraft.

Claims that the aircraft could not in-flight refuel to max weight or fly the terrain following profile under 400 feet or at heavy weights were true to the extent that these were problems that were identified in flight testing. It is precisely problems such as these that flight testing is designed to identify. A software change to the flight controls was worked out, and the mod has been tested and is being installed. This correction solves the problems and removes all restrictions.

A GAO report in 1988 claimed that down time resulting from spare part non-availability and cannibalization of aircraft to furnish parts was too high when compared to other operational systems. This was true if apples are compared to oranges, but comparing rates on a system where the parts pipeline had just started to a system which had been in existence for thirty years (B-52) or twenty years (FB-111A), hardly gives one a feeling of confidence in the evaluators. With the additional year of

Six "clamshell" mounts for ALCMs are shown underneath this aircraft. Only two B-1Bs, that are at Edwards AFB for testing, are fitted to carry the air-launched cruise missiles, and this is one of them. When carried externally on these stations, the cruise missiles affect the performance capabilities of the aircraft. Some cruise missiles can be carried internally, but the short range attack missile (SRAM) is the better option. Therefore, SRAMs are certified for the B-1B operational force.

(Simonsen via Munkasy)

experience, the rates have improved greatly, and in some instances have bettered goals.

Several of these claims got a lot of play in the fall of 1988, and since the B-1 program had been killed by one political party and revived by another, and since a presidential election was at hand, a reasonable person might conclude that politics were in truth involved in the discussion. This position is reinforced by the fact that the fixes to the problems covered above had been made or were well advanced at the time, and that information was available to those doing the sniping. Mr. Dukakis and the Democrats either lied about the B-1, or at best, failed to check readily available information about the B-1 before making false statements about it.

Some problems do exist, and they do affect the operational use of the aircraft to a degree. The need to equip the engine intake lips with an anti-icing capability stems from the fact that heating resulting from skin friction at high speed was thought to be enough to keep the ice off during normal flight. But somehow, the need to slow down to land or make practice approaches was overlooked. Someone needed to talk to the troops in the trenches on that one!

The glitch that gets all of the press is the Defensive Avionics System (DAS). From all of the pronouncements issuing forth, it seems that the survivability of the aircraft and crew is on a par with that of a kamikaze pilot in World War II. I have a problem with someone that has never penetrated anything more hazardous than the Washington beltway making pronouncements about the survivability of any penetrator--especially when they leave about seventy-five percent of the data out!

The ECM system of any penetrator is a small part of the equation since other considerations (running electronically silent, circumnavigating threats, stand-off weapons, weather, weapons effects of previous detonations, saturation tactics, corridors, and rollback to name just a few) affect the problem as well. To get an accurate picture, you cannot isolate on only one facet. The DAS was originally supposed to detect, sort by threat priority, and jam forty types of threat automatically. The system had been developed for the B-1A, and when that program was cancelled by Mr. Carter, it lay in limbo until the program was restarted. New computers and software were grafted onto the existing system to meet the threats that had evolved in the interim, but the original hardware had never received the testing it needed to make certain that it operated to specs. It did not, hence the problem. To receive all the threats specified, the receiver had to cover a wide frequency spectrum, and when it was exposed to a high threat density, it overloaded and sent confusing data to the jamming systems. Part of the problem was that the original spec was too demanding, since even with today's technology, a single system still cannot handle the task. The interim fix is to reduce the threat catalog for automatic operation to the top eleven most modern threats. A permanent fix is to add a separate receiver to cover the rest of the threats, and that is what the Air Force has proposed to Congress. In the meantime, the ill-informed critics have also forgotten that there is a Defensive Systems Officer (DSO) in the airplane that gets paid to do the same task manually as the DAS does automatically! A further factor that is overlooked is the stealth quality of the B-1B. Much has been said about the proposed B-2 stealth bomber, but the radar cross section of the B-1 is very small indeed. It must also be remembered that the best ECM system is one that stays in standby. Any time you radiate in any spectrum, you let the other guy know you are there. He may be denied good enough range and elevation data to get a lethal hit on you, but it is only a matter of time before he gets a visual or other type of fix. The experience at Red Flag has shown that the B-1B is hard to stop even in an environment where the defenders know target location, penetration corridors, and timing. The bottom line is that B-1B critics ought not to stand on the target if they want to live to a ripe old age.

PAINT SCHEMES AND MARKINGS

Much misinformation has been published about the various color schemes on the B-1 aircraft, and it has not always been an easy subject to track considering the multiple changes on the development airframes at Edwards AFB. To start with, each of the four B-1As were gloss white overall with normal size national insignia and markings. The USAF markings on the wing top and bottom, and the U.S. AIR FORCE on the fuselage sides were black instead of the usual insignia blue used on most uncamouflaged aircraft in the U.S. Air Force. The standard colors of red and yellow were used for the emergency markings. The SAC "star spangled band" on the first three ran from slightly forward of the air refueling door down through the forward quarter of the nose gear door. On number four, this band ran from just aft of the air refueling door and down through the aft quarter of the nose gear door. Numbers three and four both had the large black and white quartered circles used as targets for tracking on the outer sides of the engine nacelles for much of the time they were in the white scheme. While painted white, all four -As had black nose radomes and dielectric panels. Starting in order with number one, we find that it stayed white through all the flight testing, and only after it was placed in storage was it painted in the current dark green and gray scheme with gray national insignia of reduced size. It remains in those colors to this day at one of Griffiss Air Force Base's remote test sites. Number two stayed all white until it started the B-1B test program, at which time it picked up the red and blue trim and the B-1B TEST PROGRAM legend on the fin. Early in the B-1B testing it was repainted in the green and gray scheme with U.S. AIR FORCE on the fuselage sides and USAF on the bottom of the left wing and on the top of the right wing. Shortly after this, the markings were painted over and only the national insignia remained on each side of the aft fuselage. These insignia were black and of a reduced size. The aircraft was still in these colors and markings when it was destroyed in the crash covered

above.

Aircraft number three stayed white until ECM testing started. Then a large spine with ECM equipment was added to the fuselage top, and it was painted in a desert scheme of FS 34201, FS 30219, and Special 30400. The bottom was left in the original gloss white. This was not the Air Force Asia Minor scheme as has been reported elsewhere. Only the 30400 color is common to it and is flat instead of semi-gloss. The aircraft remained in this scheme until it was shipped to Lowry AFB where it was

The underside pattern of the Strategic Scheme is revealed in this view. Only FS 36081 and FS 36118 are used on the underside. See pages 47, 48, and 49 for drawings that illustrate the complete Strategic Scheme.

(Simonsen via Munkasy)

repainted in the current green and gray scheme. At that time the spine was removed, and it is now serving as a load trainer for munitions maintenance trainees.

Number four went from white to the desert scheme early in the flight test program, and the ECM spine was added then. The radome, like that on number three, was black to start with, but when the paint job was touched up for the visit to the Farnborough Air Show in 1982, the radome was painted in the camouflage colors. Shortly after starting B-1B testing, the spine was removed, and the radome went back to being black again. Then the aircraft was repainted in the green and gray scheme, and it remains that way at the Air Force Museum today.

The correct name for the current green and gray scheme is "Strategic Scheme," not "European One," as has been reported in other publications. This again is because of the different set of colors involved. The "Strategic Scheme" consists of FS 36081, FS 34086, and FS 36118. The 36118 has been rechecked several times since it looks lighter on the aircraft than the FS 595a chip, but it

is accurate, and it seems that the effect is due largely to the area involved and the contrast with the very dark 36081. A point to keep in mind when checking printed color patterns is the heavy blending of the fuselage at the wing glove area. This means that on a side view, the color pattern in this area is viewed nearly end on, and will be distorted. The national insignia on the bottom of the right wing is FS 36118, with the background of 36081 showing through as the star and two small bars. The national insignia on the sides of the aft fuselage are two shades of gray, with the circle and outline in a dark (36118) gray, and the star and bars in a lighter (36375) gray. Stencil markings are in light gray on dark surfaces and vice versa.

Currently all operational B-1Bs carry nose art, and while that is beyond the scope of this book, the approved colors for that artwork are black (37038), blue (35109), blue (35044), red (31136), gray (36118), gray (36081), green (34086), green (34138), brown (30111), tan (30219), and orange (32169). Whites and yellows are not to be used, but exceptions have crept in from time to time. A few examples of this art can be found on page 40.

B-1A CREW STATIONS

This is the cockpit interior of a module-equipped B-1A. The round Cathode Ray Tube (CRT) in the lower center, and the switch panel just below it, are the terrain following (TF) scope and control panel from an FB-111A. The TF scope display was later integrated into the large rectangular CRTs at each pilot station. (USAF via Bell)

The Offensive Systems Operator (OSO) station in a B-1A is shown in this photograph. The circular CRT and its associated panel is the attack radar set from the FB-111A. The display unit at the lower left is also very similar in size and configuration to that found in the FB-111A. Note the ejection handle built into the wall at the lower right corner of the photograph. (USAF via Greby)

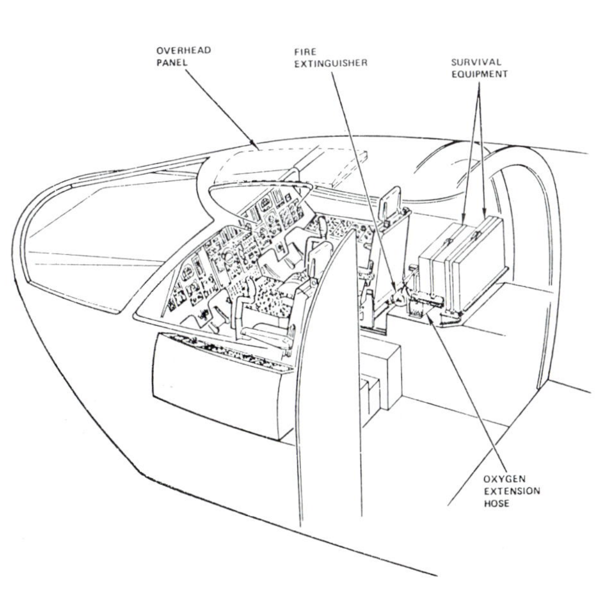

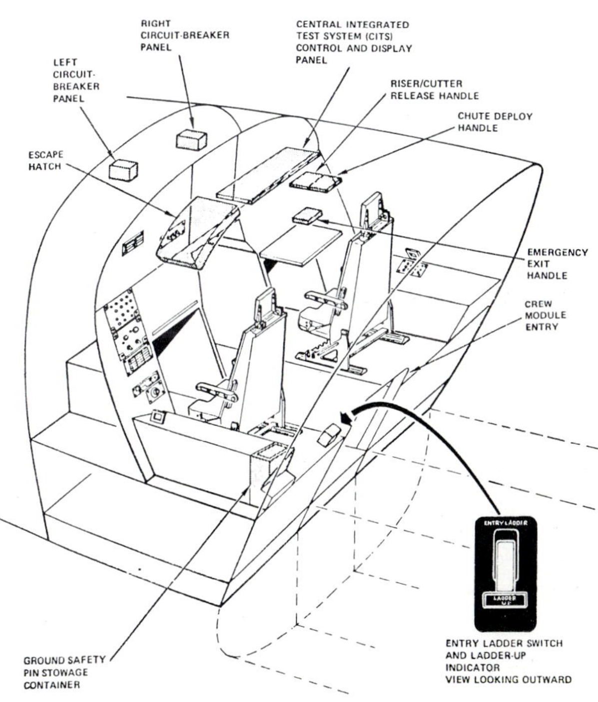

Forward crew stations in the B-1A are shown in the drawing at left, and aft crew stations are illustrated in the drawing at right. The first two B-1As had very little in the way of avionics that were permanently installed. Most of the space was used for the many items of test equipment that were removed and replaced between test runs. (USAF)

B-1B CREW & CENTRAL AVIONICS COMPARTMENTS

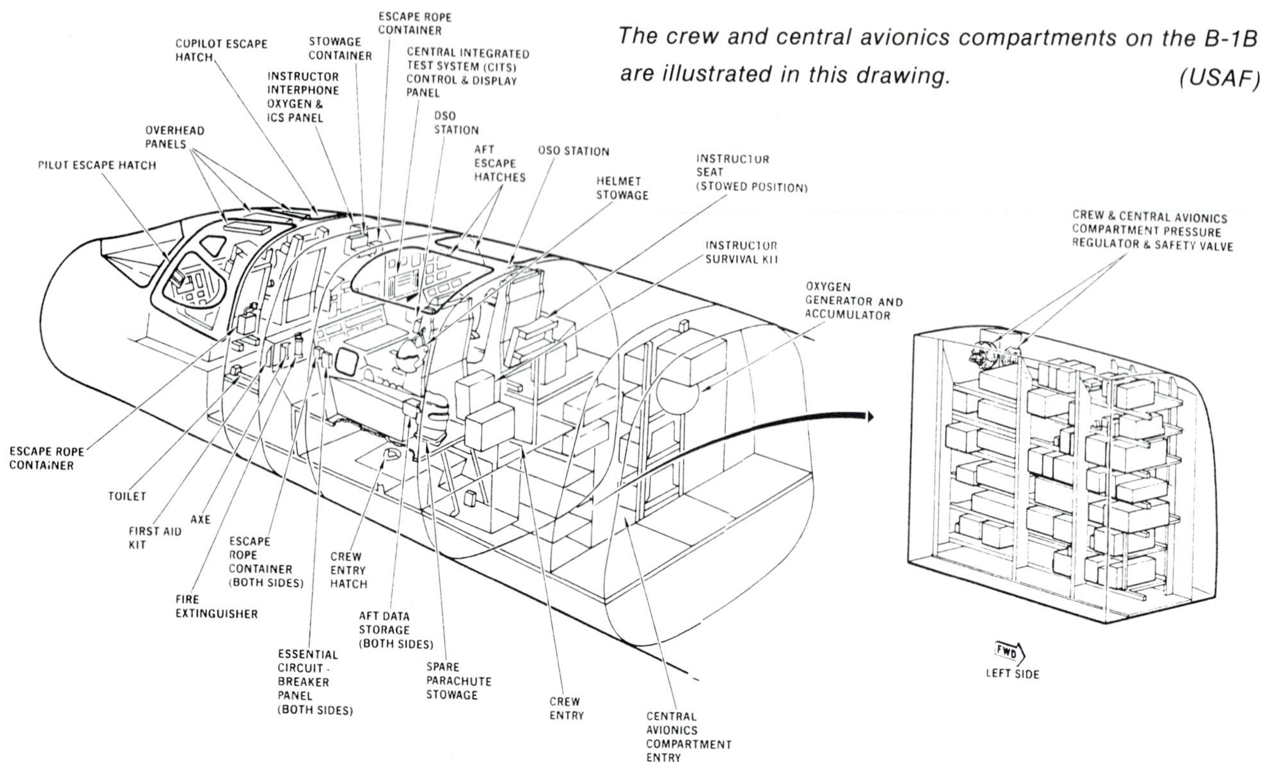

The crew and central avionics compartments on the B-1B are illustrated in this drawing.

(USAF)

B-1 MAJOR SUB-ASSEMBLY BREAKDOWN

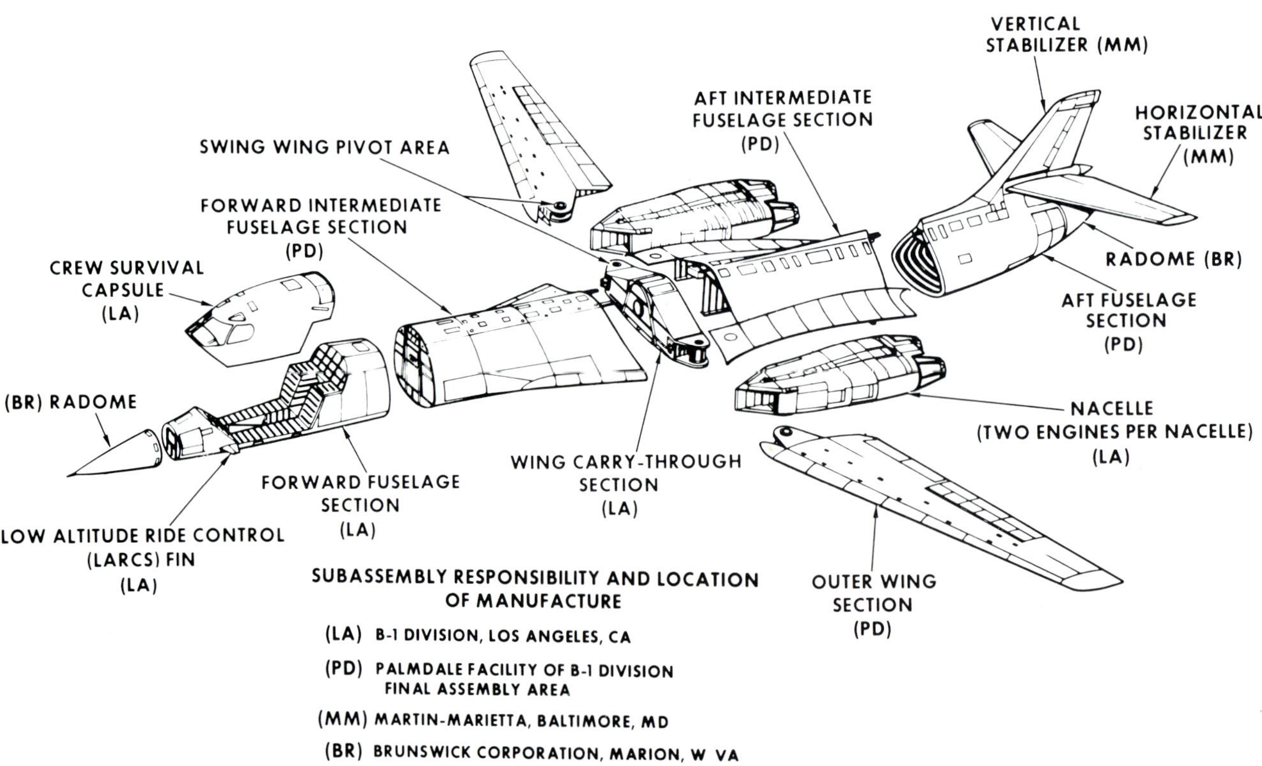

SUBASSEMBLY RESPONSIBILITY AND LOCATION OF MANUFACTURE

(LA) B-1 DIVISION, LOS ANGELES, CA

(PD) PALMDALE FACILITY OF B-1 DIVISION FINAL ASSEMBLY AREA

(MM) MARTIN-MARIETTA, BALTIMORE, MD

(BR) BRUNSWICK CORPORATION, MARION, W VA

The production responsibilities for the various subassemblies of the B-1 are shown in this drawing which was developed prior to the time when the crew escape module was deleted. Over 3,000 sub-contractors are involved with the B-1 program.

(Rockwell)

ANTENNA LOCATIONS

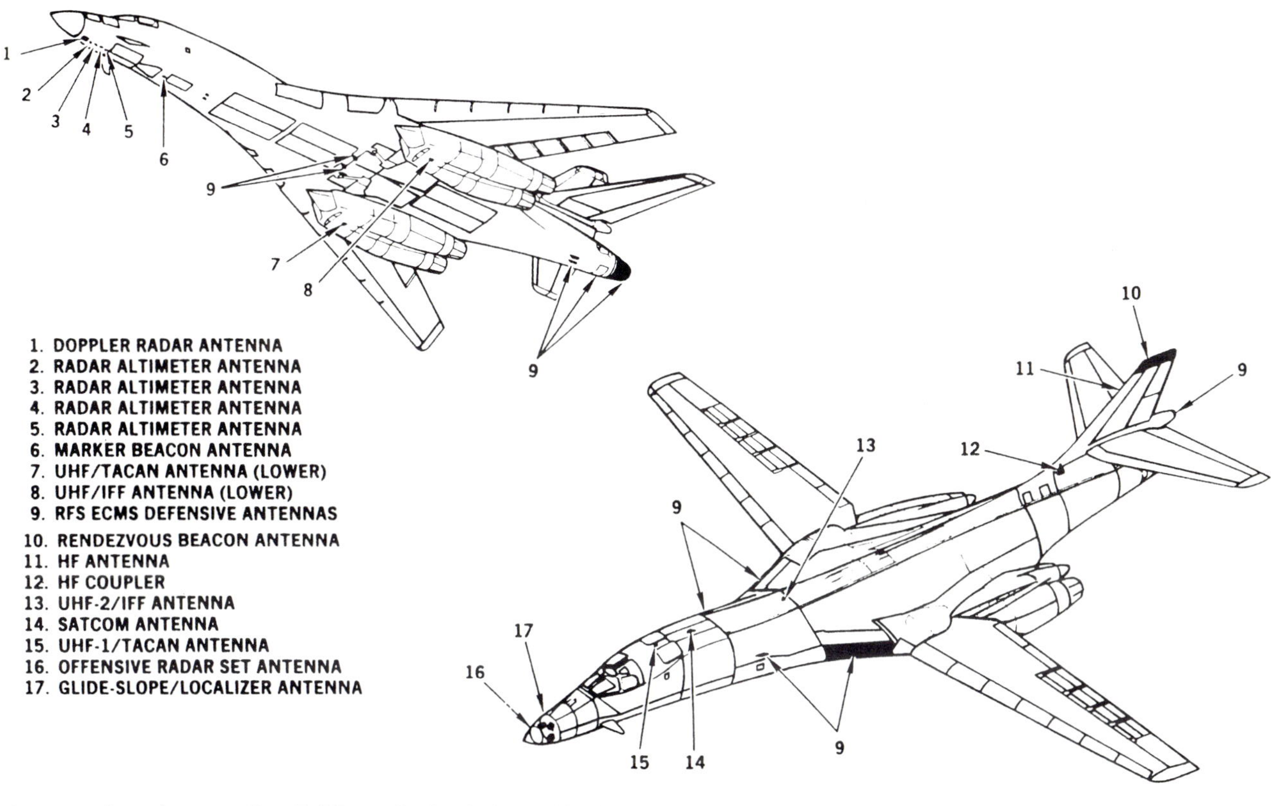

Antenna locations on the B-1B are indicated on this drawing.

(USAF)

FUEL TANK ARRANGEMENT

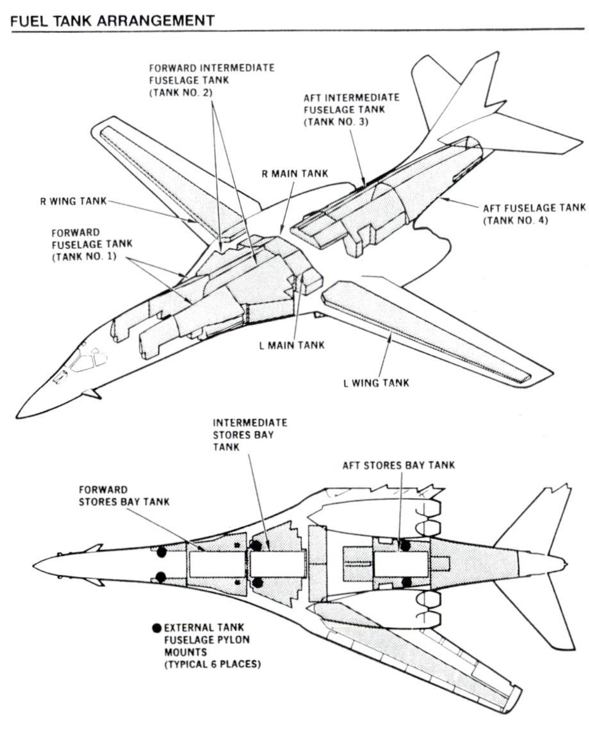

FUEL TANK QUANTITIES

TANK	FUEL QUANTITY POUNDS (GALLONS) *JP-4 (MIL-T-5624)	TOTAL FUEL AVAILABLE PER TANK	FUEL QUANTITY (ALTERNATE) POUNDS (GALLONS) **JP-5 (MIL-T-5624)	FUEL QUANTITY (EMERGENCY) ***COMBAT AUTOMOTIVE (MIL-G-3056-TYPE I)
FORWARD (NO. 1)	32,207 (4,954.9)	31,206 (4,800.9)	33,198 (4,954.9)	29,729 (4,954.9)
FORWARD INTERMEDIATE (NO. 2)	38,929 (5,989.1)	37,951 (5,838.6)	40,127 (5,989.1)	35,935 (5,989.1)
AFT INTERMEDIATE (NO. 3)	24,029 (3,696.8)	23,813 (3,663.5)	24,769 (3,696.8)	22,181 (3,696.8)
AFT (NO. 4)	52,815 (8,125.4)	51,915 (7,986.9)	54,440 (8,125.4)	48,752 (8,125.4)
MAIN	21,010 (3,232.3)	20,524 (3,157.5)	21,656 (3,232.3)	19,394 (3,232.3)
WG (L,R) (WING)	33,264 (5,117.5)	30,141 (4,637.1)	34,287 (5,117.5)	30,705 (5,117.5)
TOTAL FUEL QUANTITY	202,254 (31,116.0)	195,550 (30,084.5)	208,477 (31,116.0)	186,696 (31,116.0)
ST BAY 180 inches	19,842 (3,052.6)	19,340 (2,975.4)	20,452 (3,052.6)	18,316 (3,052.6)
91 inches	8,782 (1,351.1)	8,475 (1,303.8)	9,052 (1,351.1)	8,107 (1,351.1)

Based on Test Data — Estimated:
*Weights (volume) given is for JP-4 at Standard Day Temperature for a density of 6.5 pounds per gallon.
**Weights (volume) given is for JP-5 at Standard Day Temperature for a density of 6.7 pounds per gallon.
***Weights (volume) given is for combat automotive gasoline at Standard Day Temperature for a density of 6.0 pounds per gallon.

Locations for the fuel tanks are shown in the drawing at left, while the table at right provides quantity information for the various tanks.

(USAF)

B-1A ESCAPE MODULE

This photograph of B-1A number one was taken during tear-down, and provides a good look at the size of the escape module. The stabilization vane has been removed, leaving the white area underneath clearly visible.

(USAF via Hjort)

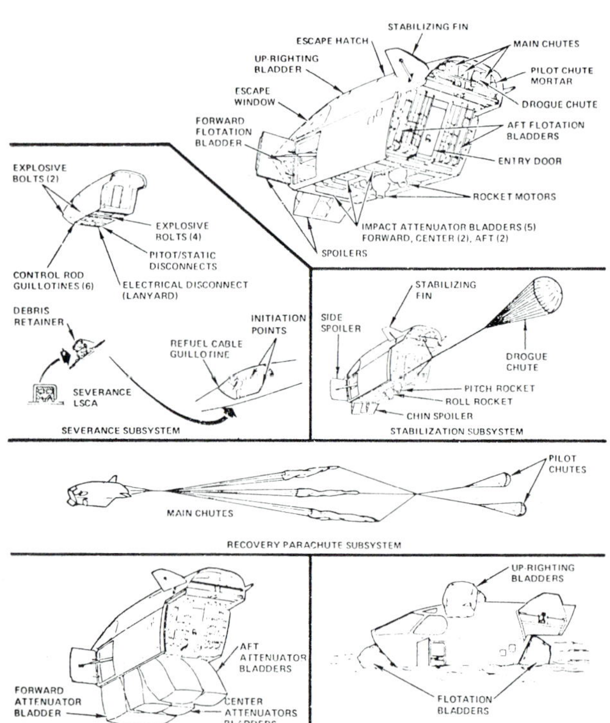

The crew escape module was a large complex system itself, and when it proved to be unstable at ejection speeds above 350 knots, the only option was to use ejection seats for all subsequent airframes. *(USAF)*

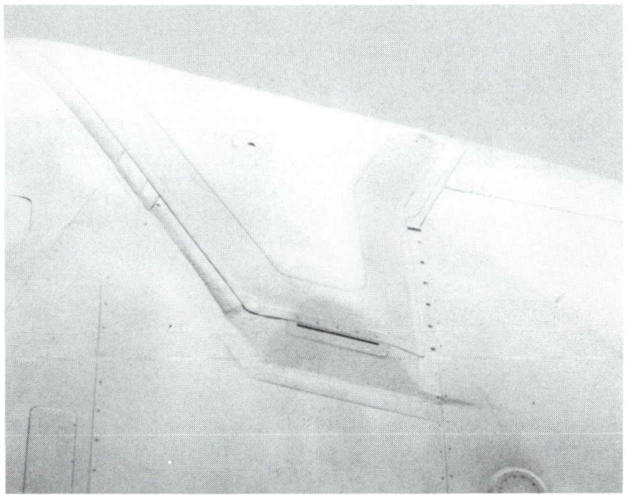

B-1As one, two, and three, that were equipped with the crew escape module, had large stabilization vanes on either side of the module/fuselage. Even in the stowed or retracted position, these vanes stood proud of the fuselage as shown here. This is the vane on the left side. The vanes extended automatically as part of the ejection sequence, but had to be raised manually for access to the central avionics compartment which was located beneath them. When they were eliminated, the fuselage was redesigned for better interior access for maintenance. This was a plus for the northern bases in winter. *(Greby)*

SEATS

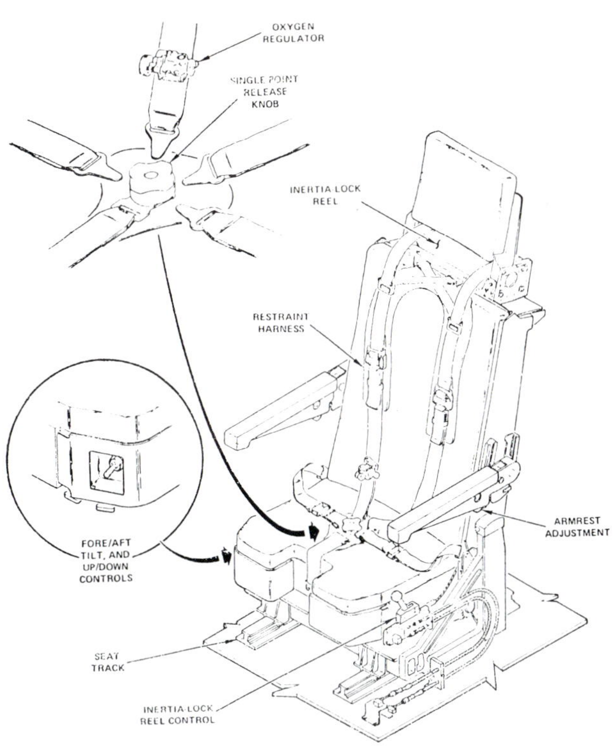

No complexity was involved in the seats that were used in module-equipped aircraft. *(USAF)*

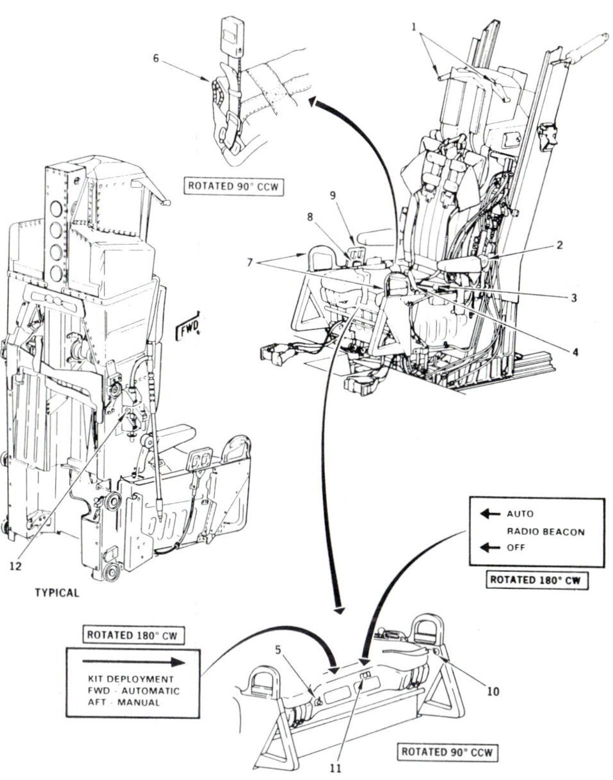

The ACES II seats in the B-1B are modified for operation where ejection through a hatch is necessary. The seat incorporates limb restraints to avoid occupant injury on the edges of the hatch opening as the seat ejects. This drawing shows the details of the seat as used in the B-1B. *(USAF)*

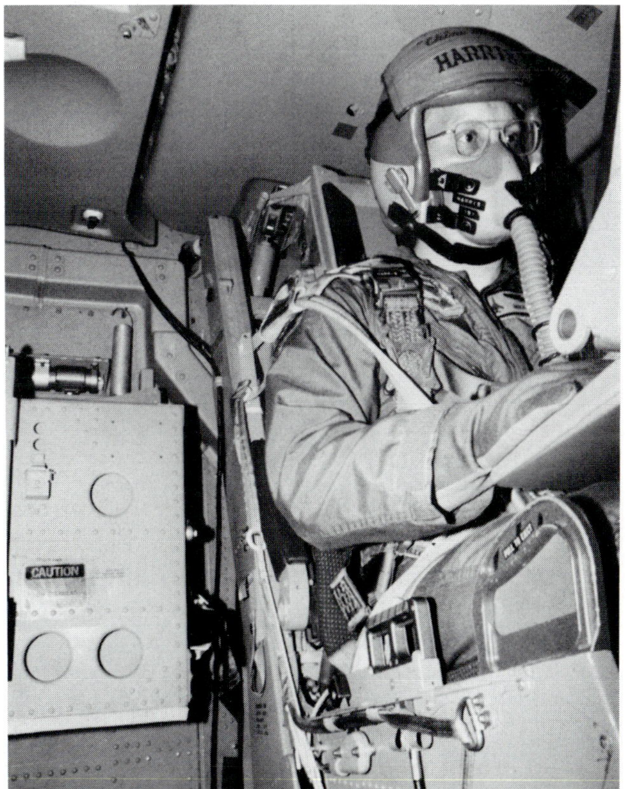

The arm restraint net is stowed at the side of the seat with attachment points at the "D" ring under the ejection handle and behind the shoulder of the seat occupant. Note the hatch above the seat and the minimal clearance that exists. *(Zaloga)*

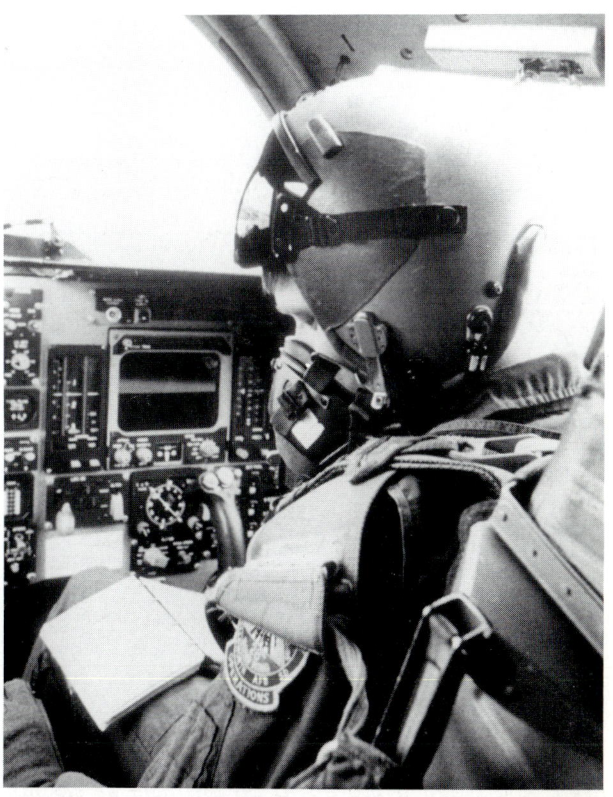

The epaulet on the shoulder harness is one of the anchors for the arm restraint net. *(Zaloga)*

LANDING GEAR DETAIL

This front view of the nose gear well on B-1A number one shows the drag link attachment point and the mechanism that opens and closes the doors.   (USAF via Hjort)

The nose landing gear of B-1A number one is shown here from the front and slightly to the left. One of the landing lights is missing a bulb, and the other is completely gone. The long drag link used on the first three B-1As is visible.
                                              (USAF via Hjort)

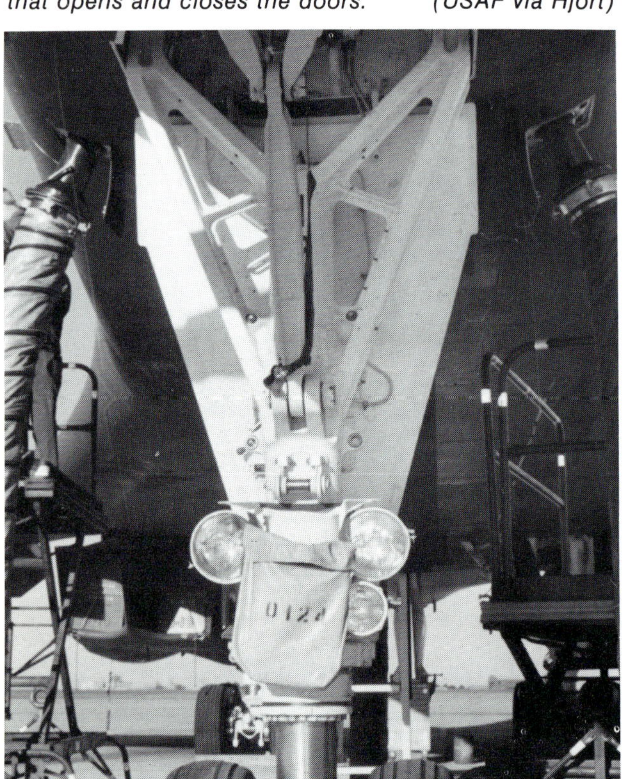

B-1A number four and all B-1Bs have the short drag link, but with that exception, the nose gear and well are very similar to that used on the first three B-1As. The bag hung on the lights holds the aircraft's maintenance forms.

This is the nose gear of a B-1B as viewed from the left side.

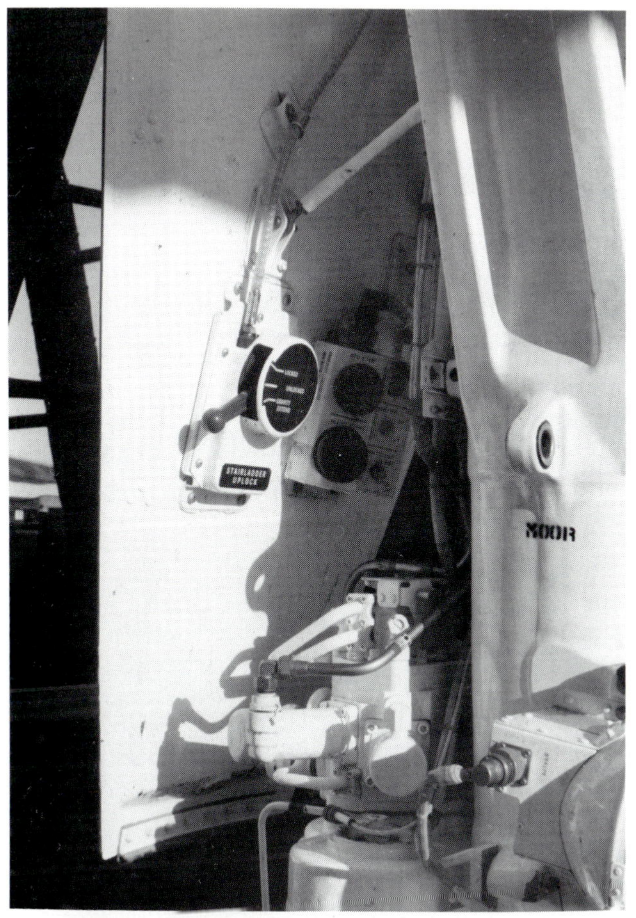

Details of the nose wheel on a B-1B are shown here. The only visible difference between this wheel and the one used on the B-1As is that the wheel on the B-1A was painted black except for the small cap in the center, which was white. (K. Wachsmuth)

Left: This close-up view of the right side of the nose landing gear strut and aft door shows the manual control for the entry stairladder and the electrical controls for the stairladder, main gear doors, and alert start. One of the two rods that attach the aft door to the strut is also visible.

This view looks straight up into the aft section of the nose gear well. Forward is to the top of the photograph. Just visible to the right of the drag link is one of the retraction actuators. The 4,000 PSI hydraulic system means that smaller actuators can be used, thus saving weight.

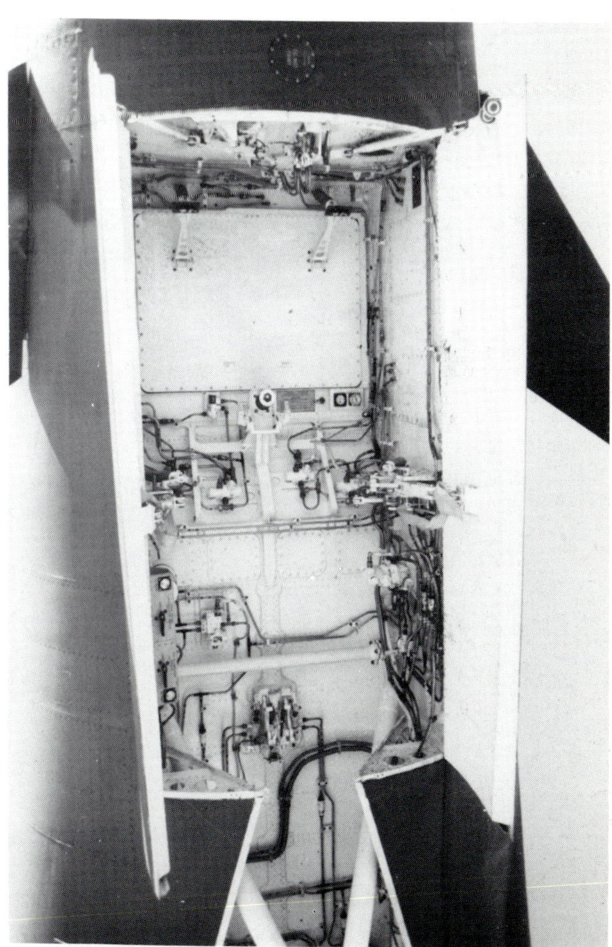

This is the forward portion of the nose gear well. Gear wells are painted white, as are the struts and the insides of the doors. Note the door actuators at the mid-point and the small brace rods at the forward end.

This is a head-on view of the main gear with the large doors open and locks installed to prevent their inadvertent closure. This is the normal configuration when the aircraft is on the ground during pre and post-flight inspections. Note the two RFS/ECMS antennas just forward of the gear well.

With the engine nacelles removed, more details of the main landing gear struts are visible in this photograph. Aft is to the right.   (Greby)

Main wheels on the B-1As were black with the anti-skid unit cover being white. Note that the center is raised rather than being flat as on the main gear wheel on the B-1B shown in the photo at right. The small white disc on each wheel near the bolts is a pressure gage.

The main strut and braces for the left main gear are seen here from the front and the inside.

Main gear wheels on the B-1B are white with a different hole and bolt pattern than that used on the B-1A. Note also the sharply raked UHF/IFF antenna on the underside of the nacelle.

This is a front view of the main strut and wheels. Note the gage mounted on the strut to measure inflation of the oleo-pneumatic shock absorber.

This view looks forward into the right main gear well on B-1A number one. Note the many test cable runs and stiffeners that extend into the well. Also of interest is the partially open position of the two forward weapons bays.
(USAF via Hjort)

This view looks vertically up into the right main gear well. The left well is essentially a mirror image. Forward is to the top of this photograph.

The right main gear well on a B-1B is shown here. The photograph is taken from behind the gear and looks forward.

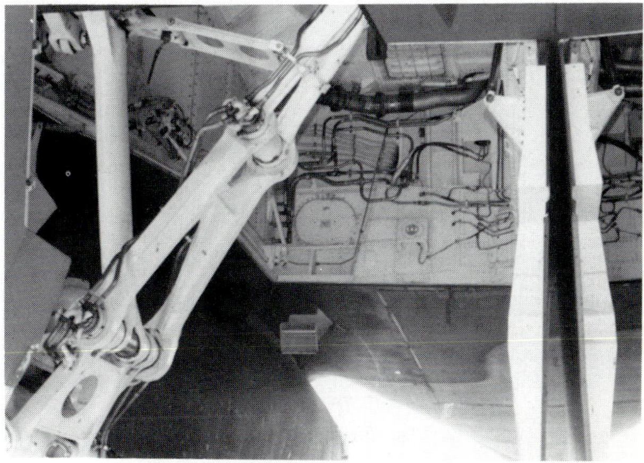

Details of the aft portion of the right main gear well on a B-1B are illustrated here. The photo looks up and aft.

ENGINE DETAILS

This impressive shot, taken at night, shows the four engines on a B-1B being run up for tests.

(Simonsen via Munkasy)

Open access doors on the engine bay panels of a B-1B show the ease of access and the white color of all interior components.

Left: The exhaust doors for the auxiliary power unit are on the bottoms of the nacelles, and are usually missed. The paint on the doors rapidly scorches and burns.

Above: The left nacelle on B-1A number one is shown in this view. From this angle, it looks very much like one of the engine fairings on the F-101 Voodoo--only much larger! (USAF)

Right: The F101 engine is a compact unit producing 17,000 pounds of thrust at military power and 30,000 pounds in full afterburner. It is installation neutral, meaning that it can be installed in any of the four positions without the need for adapters.

Below: The fan bypass air on the F101 exhausts into the tailpipe in the afterburner section, giving it a leaner burn in afterburner. This results in a reduced IR plume in non-afterburning power settings. This cut-away view of the engine reveals its major components. (General Electric)

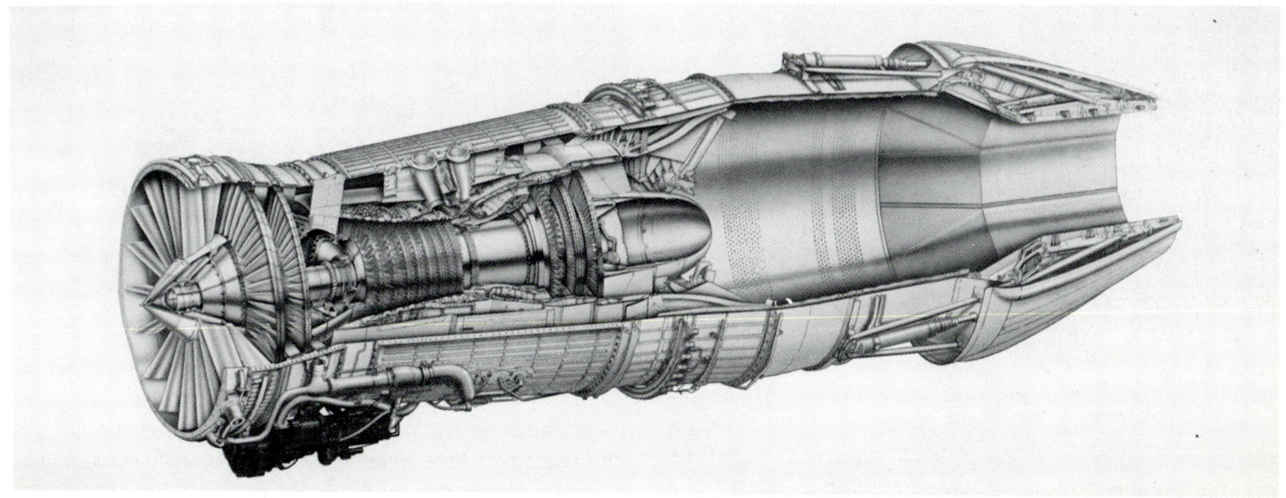

Details of the intake on the left nacelle of B-1A number three are shown here. These include the ramp required to allow speeds in excess of Mach 2. Note the pitot tubes just forward of the ramp and under the intake. The side intake lips are spread to increase capture area at low speeds. (Greby)

A side view of the intake on a B-1A shows the vertical forward edge of the central flow divider and the aft-facing outlets under the intake chin. (Greby)

Above: The intakes on the B-1B differ from those on the prototypes. This head-on view shows a solid flow divider and no pitots. The hinged lips are retained, and are open when the landing gear handle is in the down position.

Right: This close-up of a B-1B intake shows the radar cross section (RCS) vanes that provide a serpentine path through the intake. This prevents radar reflection from the compressor face, and adds to the stealth quality of the B-1B. The object lying on the bottom of the lip is the folded intake plug. Note the bulge along the lower side of the nacelle and the antenna just aft of the lower lip.

This is the aft portion of the left nacelle on a B-1B. Compare this to the similar photograph of B-1A number one on page 26. Note the differences in nozzle length and the configuration of the nozzle actuator fairing. The treatment of the hinges and latches is aerodynamically cleaner than on the B-1A.

The exhaust area for the left nacelle on B-1A number three is shown here with the engines removed. B-1A numbers one and two were the same as this. Note the boat tail fairing between the engines, and the lack of any exhaust for the bleed air system's air-to-air cooler.

(Greby)

A top rear view of the left engine nacelle on B-1A number four reveals the circular exhaust for the bleed air system's air-to-air cooler. This configuration was only on B-1A number four.

The flame holders can be seen in this view that looks into the interiors of the tailpipes of the two right engines on a B-1B. The inner tips of the flame holders have a white ceramic-like coating. Note also the rectangular shape of the air-to-air cooler exhaust as used on the B-1B. Just visible between the tailpipes is the small aerodynamic guide vane that aids the airflow transition around the exhausts.

(Bishop)

Here is the same guide vane as photographed from the front. Also of interest is the lip where the nacelle transitions to the nozzle actuator fairing.

NOSE, RADOME, & RADAR DETAILS

This is the nose section on B-1A number three. Note the "double cone" effect of the radome, and compare the fuselage length forward of the windshield with that of the B-1B in the photograph at right. Other differences are the rake of the windshield pillar and the position of the Structural Mode Central System (SMCS) vane. (Greby)

The nose section of a B-1B is shown here for comparison to the photograph of B-1A number three at left. The longer forward avionics bay is evident, as is the shorter ogival-shaped radome. Note the angle of the windshield pillar, and that the SMCS vane is about a foot further forward. (Zaloga)

This view of B-1A number four shows the early finish on the doppler antenna, the two pitot tubes, and two yaw sensors under the nose.

Another photograph of the same area on a B-1B shows the left three of six pitot tubes common to B-1B number nineteen and subsequent. Earlier B-1Bs have only the lower two tubes on each side. The two small projections at the five and seven o'clock positions are temperature probes.

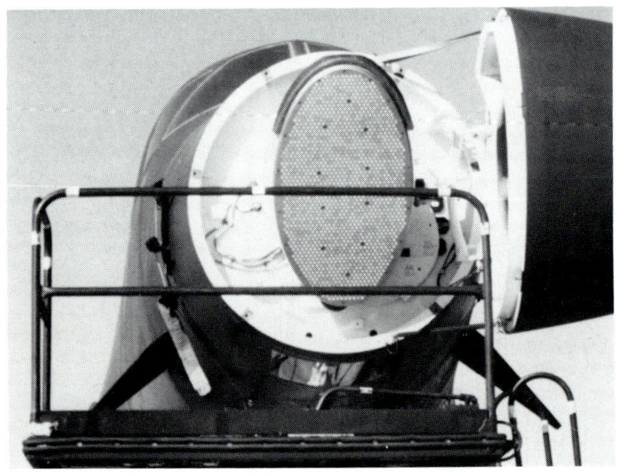

With the radome open, the antenna for the AN/APQ-164 offensive radar system is visible. The unit is a modification of the AN/APG-68 used in the F-16, and combines navigation, weapons aiming, and terrain following functions in one unit.

A side view of the ORS radar antenna shows additional details. The antenna can rotate on the pedestal to look to the side in a high resolution mode in order to take fixes on points off of the aircraft's track.

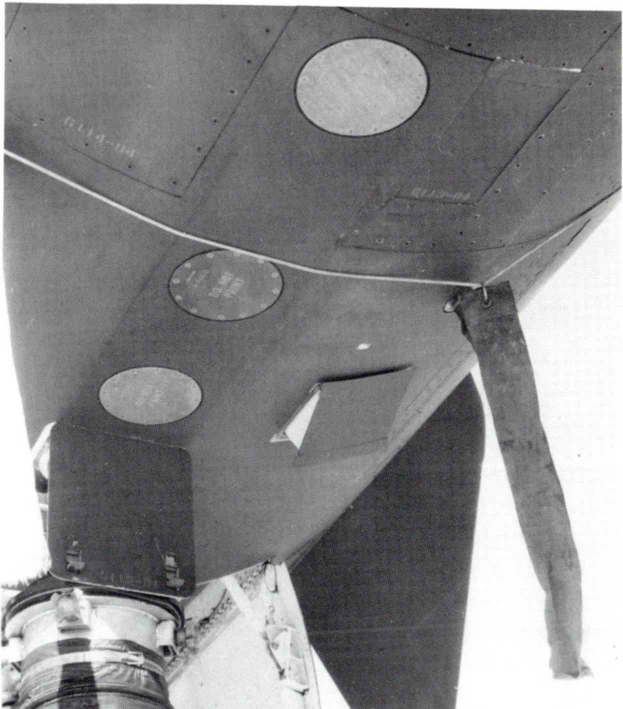

The shiny panel under the nose is the doppler radar antenna, and the circular plates are radar altimeter antennas. The color of the doppler antenna is FS 16081, a gloss finish of the dark gray camouflage color. The three lines on the ORS radome are metal grounding wires that conduct static electrical charges to the airframe.

A close-up of the radar altimeter antennas shows three of the four, with the other one being behind the cooling duct. They are a dark gray metallic color.

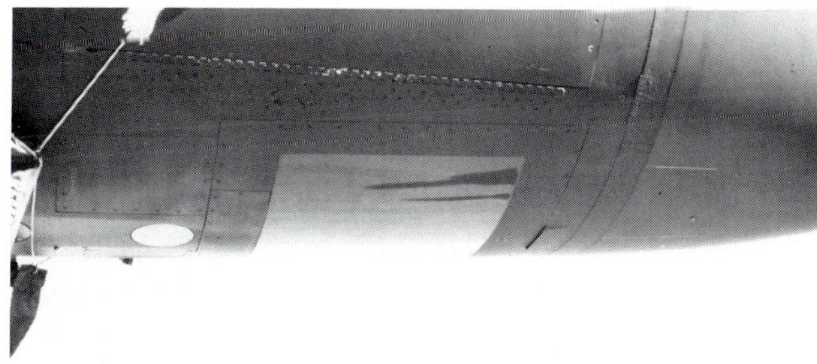

This view shows the small cooling air exhaust just aft of the ORS radome, and the flat fuselage section where the radar altimeter antennas are mounted.

The definitive refueling markings are white and similar to the black markings on B-1B number one at roll-out.

The refueling receptacle door is shown here in the open position. Note the beating this area takes from the boom nozzle during the attempts to make contact.

ENTRY STAIRLADDER

The entry stairladder will extend or retract using aircraft power, or it may be extended by gravity. The stairladder is white except for the black anti-skid steps. In the photograph at right, note the two cooling air exhausts located on each side of the ladder.

EXTERIOR LIGHTING

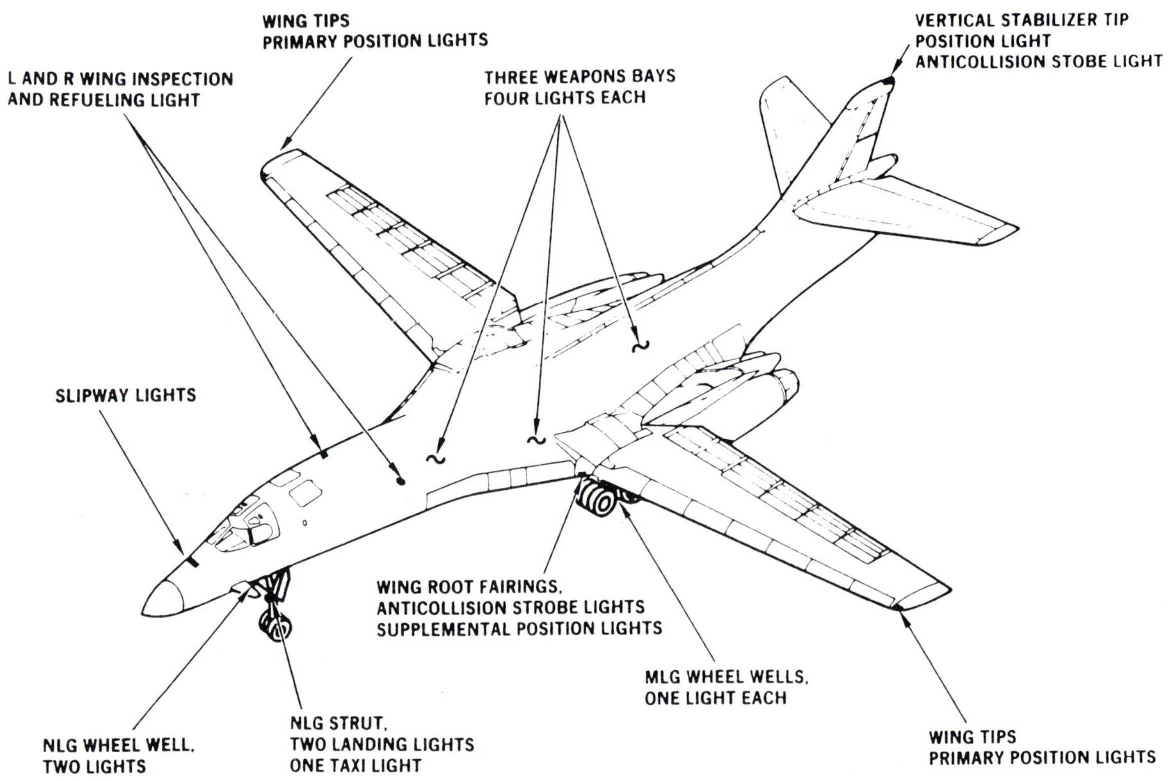

Coverage of the B-1's details continues on page 52.

COLOR GALLERY   B-1A NUMBER 1

Taken on October 26, 1974, this photograph shows the first B-1A at Rockwell's Palmdale plant. Note the Rockwell logo on the vertical tail, and the stabilization fins on the crew module.   (Brewer)

This in-flight view of B-1A number one shows the boundary air exits under the nacelles.   (Morris via Brewer)

B-1A number one was painted in the green/gray camouflage scheme after testing was finished. Note the missing fin cap and the fact that the long pitot boom still remains on the nose.   (Logan via Brewer)

B-1A NUMBER 2

B-1A number two was photographed on November 12, 1977, at Edwards Air Force Base. It was first used as a structural test aircraft, then was added to the flight test program. Its all white scheme was identical to that on number one except for the tail number and the large 2 on the nose gear door. (Brewer)

Later, a large B-1B test logo was added to the vertical tail of number two after it and number four had begun testing for the B-1B program. (USAF DF-ST-83-08064)

These two photographs show B-1A number two after it was painted in the green/gray Strategic Scheme. It was still in these colors when it was destroyed in the aft CG accident on August 29, 1984. (Left USAF DF-SC-84-10514, right Logan via Brewer)

B-1A NUMBER 3

B-1A number three is shown here in its original overall gloss white scheme. This photograph was taken at Edwards AFB on November 12, 1977. The short pitot tube is the only obvious change from the first two prototypes. *(Brewer)*

The second scheme to be applied to B-1A number three was the desert camouflage illustrated here. The ECM fairing was added to the spine of the aircraft. Note the raised stabilization vane on the crew escape module. This photo is dated July 28, 1984. *(Sveinsson via Brewer)*

Dated July 25, 1989, this photograph shows B-1A number three in its current Strategic Scheme. It is at Lowry AFB, Colorado, where it is used as a munitions upload trainer. *(Greby)*

INTERIOR COLORS

Colors of the main instrument panel in B-1B, 86-0124, are illustrated here.

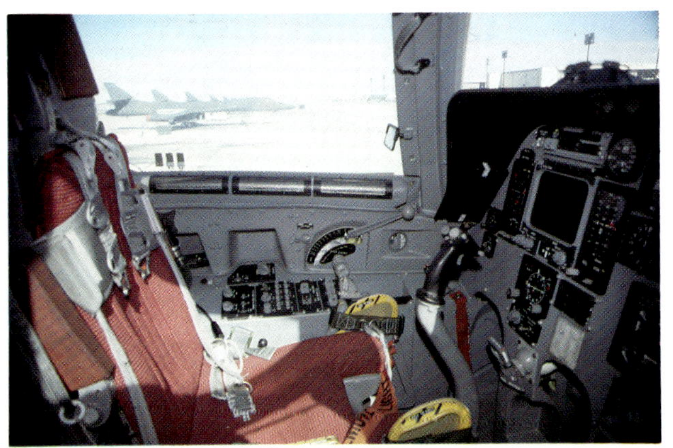

Center left: This is the pilot's seat and side panel. Note the wing sweep handle just under the window and the ejection leg restraint garters looped over the seat handles.

Center right: The copilot's seat and side panel are illustrated in this photo.

Left: This is the overhead switch panel. The two circular objects just below it at the front are ventilation air outlets.

Controls and three CRT displays at the DSO's station are seen in this view. The work table rotates up automatically as part of the ejection sequence.

The OSO's station is shown here with the Offensive Radar System in operation. A low altitude display can be seen on the scope. *(Zaloga)*

These two photographs were taken in a maintenance trainer, and show details of the DSO (left) and OSO (right) panels. The pushbutton, seen in both photographs below the center panel, is only in the trainer.

This is the OSO's seat. Note the epaulets on the shoulder straps and the leg restraint garter stowed over the ejection handle.

Details of the DSO's seat are shown here. Just aft of the ejection handle and under the "Remove Before Flight" streamer is the arm restraint net. It is attached to the "D" ring on the side of the seat.

B-1A NUMBER 4

B-1A number four can be identified by the large dielectric panels on the wing glove and the lack of module stabilization vanes. It is shown here in July 1979 in its original overall white scheme. (McNeil via Brewer)

These two views show B-1A number four after it was painted in the desert camouflage scheme and the ECM fairing was added to the spine. The nose radome was painted to match the desert scheme for the Farnborough visit. Note the dielectric panels on the wing glove and the rounded aft radome. This was the only B-1A to have this configuration. (Left USAF DF-ST-82-08092, right USAF DF-ST-82-0891)

With B-1B radomes and the Strategic Scheme, B-1A number four is identifiable by its raised spoilers and the square engine inlet profile. (Logan via Brewer)

B-1B COLORS

This high angle view shows the subdued markings to good effect. The simpler white refueling markings are clearly illustrated.
(USAF DF-ST-88-07183)

The pattern of the camouflage scheme on the underside shows up well in this photograph that was taken while the aircraft was in a roll. Fuel is exiting through the jettison outlets. Note the white interior color showing through the gaps around the weapons bays and main gear doors.
(USAF DF-ST-88-07193)

B-1B NOSE ART

Nose art now adorns operational B-1Bs. On this page is a representative sample of some of that art. At left is the "Star of Abilene," 83-0065, in its present, mostly subdued colors. At right is the design on B-1B, 86-0124, at McConnell AFB. It was the winner in a state wide "nose art" contest.　　　*(Left USAF, right Bishop)*

The aircraft shown in the top right photograph is shown again in this view. These are the present colors used on the aircraft, which was the first B-1B to visit the United Kingdom.　　　*(Bishop)*

This is "Heavy Metal," 85-0078, photographed in May 1989, at Ellsworth Air Force Base.　　　*(Zaloga)*

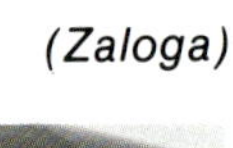

B-1B, 85-0085, is "America 1."　　　*(Zaloga)*

"Ghost Rider" is B-1B, 86-0069.　　　*(Zaloga)*

At left is "Freedom 1," 86-0098, and at right is "Gremlin," which is 85-0087.　　　*(Both Zaloga)*

DIMENSIONS

MEASUREMENT	ACTUAL DIMENSION	1/144TH SCALE	1/72ND SCALE	1/48TH SCALE
Wingspan (unswept)	136' 8.5"	11.39"	22.78"	34.17"
Wingspan (swept)	78' 2.5"	6.51"	13.03"	19.55"
Length (B-1A 3 & 4 with pitot)	150' 2.5"	12.51"	25.03"	37.55"
Length (B-1B)	147'	12.25"	24.50"	36.75"
Height at top of vertical fin*	34'	2.83"	5.60"	11.20"

* Height measurements will vary depending on tire pressure and the amount of fuel and weapons bay stores loaded.

B-1A & B-1B SCALE DRAWINGS

ALL DRAWINGS ON PAGES 41 THROUGH 51 ARE 1/200th SCALE

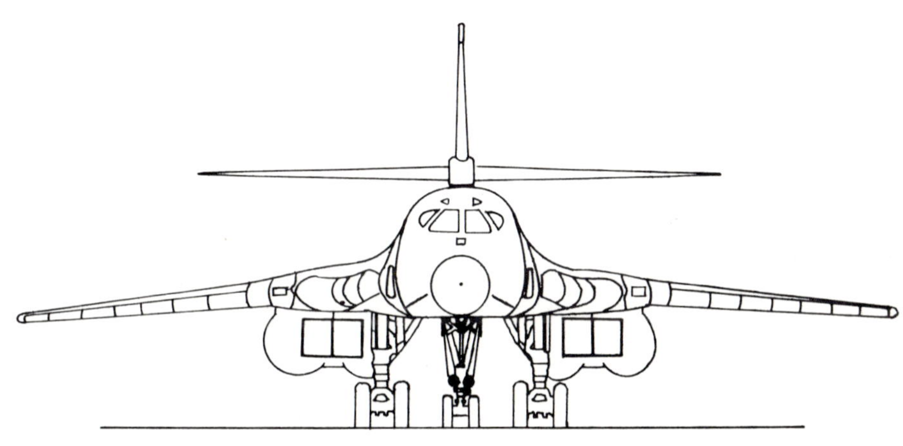

Wayne Wachsmuth

B-1B FRONT VIEW

The front view is shown with the wings swept for space considerations. The only noticeable differences that can be observed from this angle between the B-1A and B-1B are the cabin exhaust/chute bridle fairlead on top of the fuselage and the longer nose gear drag link.

VENTS & INTAKES

On the module-equipped B-1As, the exhaust for the cabin and avionics cooling and pressurization air was on the centerline just aft of the eyebrow windows. Running through the center of the duct was the fairing for the parachute bridle that ripped through sheet metal as the module repositioned to a level attitude for landing. The tape in the foreground covers the attachment point for the ultra high frequency (UHF) number one and the tactical air navigation (TACAN) antenna.

On B-1A number four (illustrated in this photo) and all B-1Bs, the cabin and avionics cooling and pressurization vent was moved aft and to the left of centerline. The circular panel is the satellite communication (SATCOM) antenna that is in the same position on the B-1Bs. However, it is rectangular in shape on the -Bs.

Left: The avionics cooling air exhaust on all B-1Bs is on the right side, even with the front of bay number one. It is open when the aircraft is on the ground and any power is applied to the avionics.

Center right: Cooling air exhausts on the B-1B are located on each side of the entry stairladder. On B-1A number four, the location was the same, but the configuration was a set of flush louvers rather than being vents as shown here. On the first three B-1As, the exhausts were louvered outlets that were located at the front corners of bay number one.

The fuel jettison outlets on each wing were in a trailing edge notch only on B-1A number one.

On B-1A number two and all subsequent aircraft, the fuel jettison outlets or vents were this configuration.

Intake scoops for the fuel/air coolers are located just aft of the main gear well and inboard of the nacelle on each side. This scoop is shown in the closed position.

An open fuel/air cooler scoop is shown here. These are frequently open when the aircraft is on the ground. Note the white interior color and the slight overspray of the exterior color.

Right: The circular vent aft of the national insignia is for the fuel tanks, and is only on the right side. Note the three missing vortex generators.

RFS & ECMS

The large dielectric panels on the wing glove area were on B-1A number four and the B-1Bs. On B-1A number four, they were very noticeable, because they were black in color. This contrasted against the original white paint scheme and the desert camouflage as shown here.

(Rockwell via Munkasy)

On B-1Bs, the dielectric panels are less noticeable because they are the same color as one of the camouflage colors, but their outline is still visible.

(Rockwell via Munkasy)

RFS/ECMS DEFENSIVE AVIONICS SYSTEM

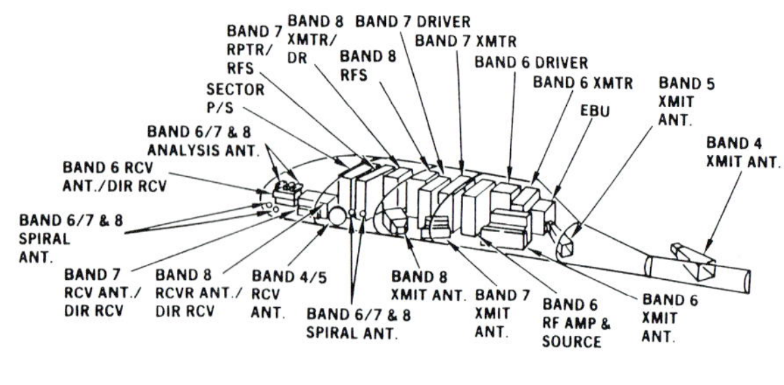

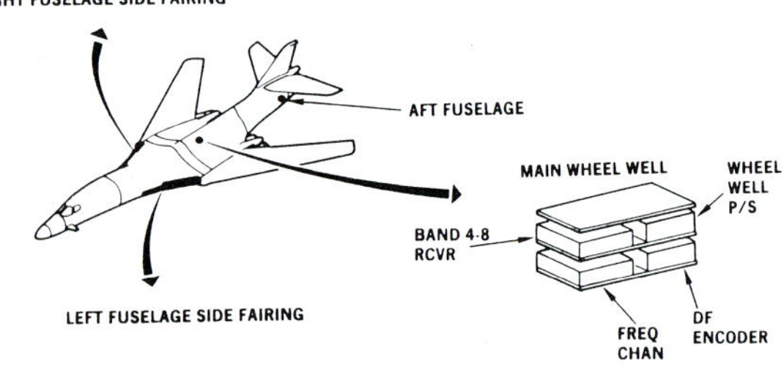

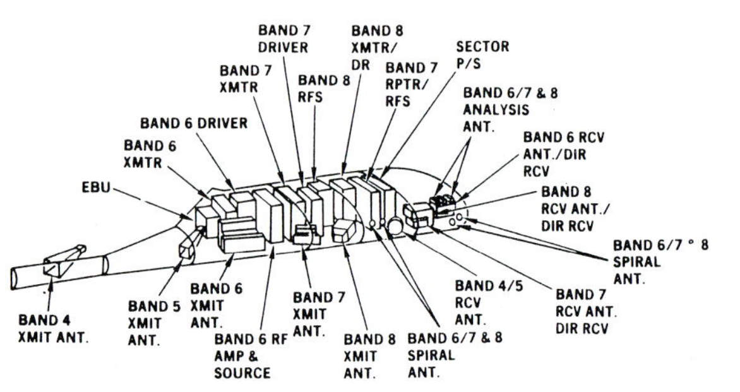

This photo, taken from a different angle, shows the texture of the dielectric panels to good effect. Note the areas where the colors of the paint overlap, giving a different value to the finish.

This large RFS blade antenna is on the top of the fuselage of B-1A number four. One is mounted on each side, just forward of the light used to illuminate the upper surface of the wing during air refuelings at night. On the spine, and partly obscured by the missile in the background, is the blade antenna for the UHF radio number two, and the IFF system.

A pointed tail cone was used on the first three B-1As as seen here on B-1A number three. It was shaped more for aerodynamic than equipment considerations. Note the pointed fairing extending aft from the joint between the stabilators and the vertical fin/rudder. (Greby)

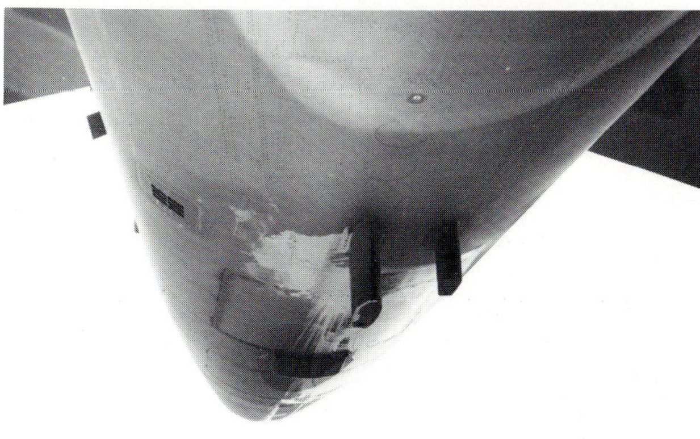

In addition to the two large RFS antennas just forward of the main gear well, there are two more under the tail section. The cooling air outlet, visible to the left, is duplicated on the other side of the fuselage.

Beginning with B-1B number nineteen, a sharply raked RFS antenna was introduced. Note that the UHF/IFF antenna is also raked. The dielectric panels on the wing glove have a different texture than the rest of the aircraft, because they come with special paint and are masked when the aircraft is painted. All dielectric panels and radomes are treated the same way.

This right side view shows the B-1B tail cone that houses the RFS/ECMS receiving and transmitting antennas. Note the large vortex generators.

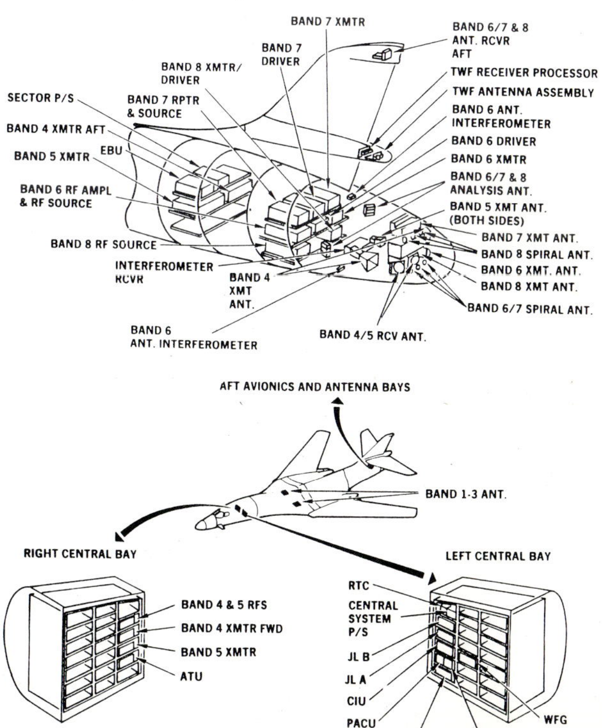

The fin cap on the B-1B houses ECMS receivers and the rendezvous beacon antenna. It also serves as a mount for the white tail light and an anti-collision strobe light. The lights are the same in either case, but compare the shape of this fin cap to the one used on B-1A numbers one and two as illustrated in the photograph at right.

This fairing on the B-1B contains the tail warning radar, and it is not only blunt, but continues the almost square cross section of the fairing between the stabilators and vertical fin to its tip. Compare this to the pointed fairing with a circular cross section that was used on the first three prototypes. It is illustrated on the previous page.

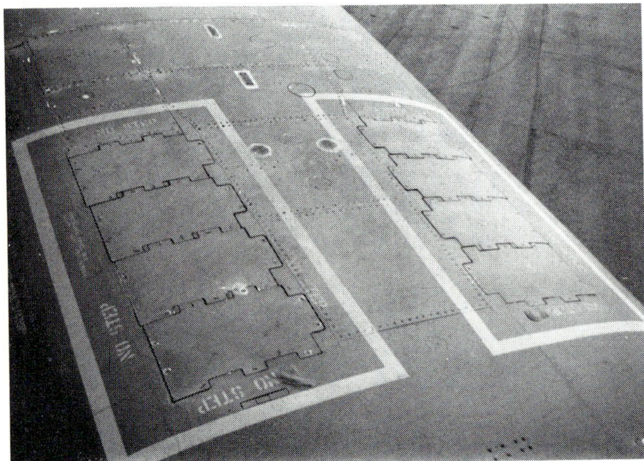

The covers for the expendable countermeasures (EXCM) are frangible and are blown away when chaff or flares are dispensed.

B-1As numbers one and two had no ECM gear, and the fin cap was shaped for aerodynamics.

EXCM DISPENSERS

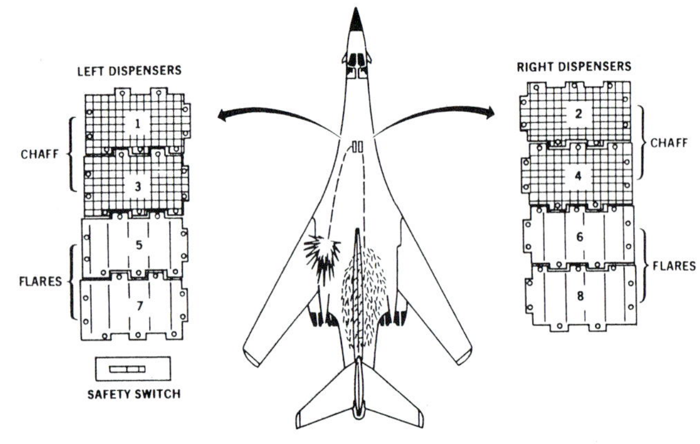

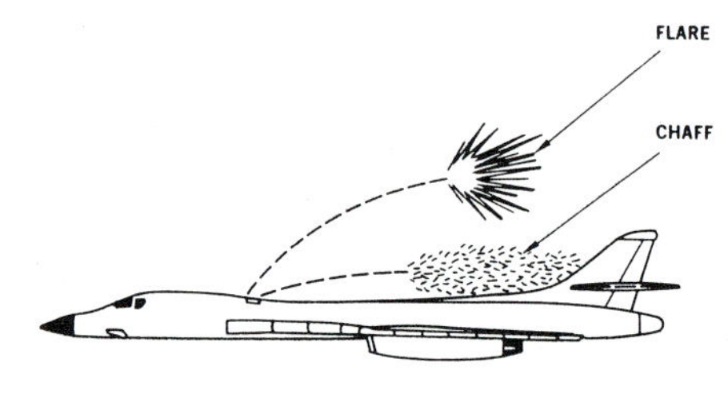

This drawing shows the operation of the EXCM system.
(USAF)

WEAPONS BAYS

The white interior color of the weapons bays show through gaps in the doors, and outline their locations on the underside of the aircraft.
(Rockwell via Munkasy)

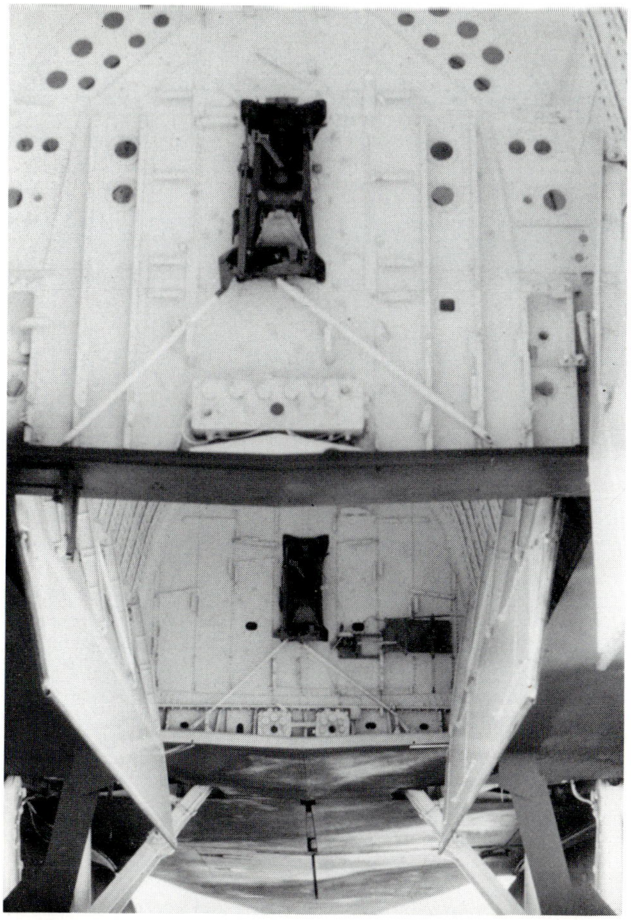

At left is a view looking aft into bays one and two on B-1A number three. The photograph at right looks forward into the same bays. The shape of the bays is apparent, as are the numerous holes that were filled with cables during testing.
(Both Greby)

The forward end of bay two in a B-1B is shown here. This bulkhead is moveable on the B-1B to lengthen the bay for carriage of longer weapons. At bottom center is the spoiler that extends when the doors open to reduce turbulence inside the bay. The lever protruding at right is a bay door safety interlock that prevents inadvertent operation of the doors.

This is the aft end of bay two on a B-1B. The darker colored tubes with the spiral bands are wing sweep and flap/slat interconnect torque tubes.

Center left: This photograph looks forward in bay three of a B-1B. The doors are a graphite composite construction with hinges and fittings being made of metal.

Center right: The aft end of bay three is shown here. On operational B-1Bs, weapons are carried in bays two and three, and a fuel tank is carried in bay one.

Right: The underside of a B-1B is seen here with the bay doors closed. Note the safety interlock levers and the gaps at the edges of the doors that allows the white interior color to show through. The line where the doors on bay one split to make bay two longer is visible.

WEAPONS BAY STORES

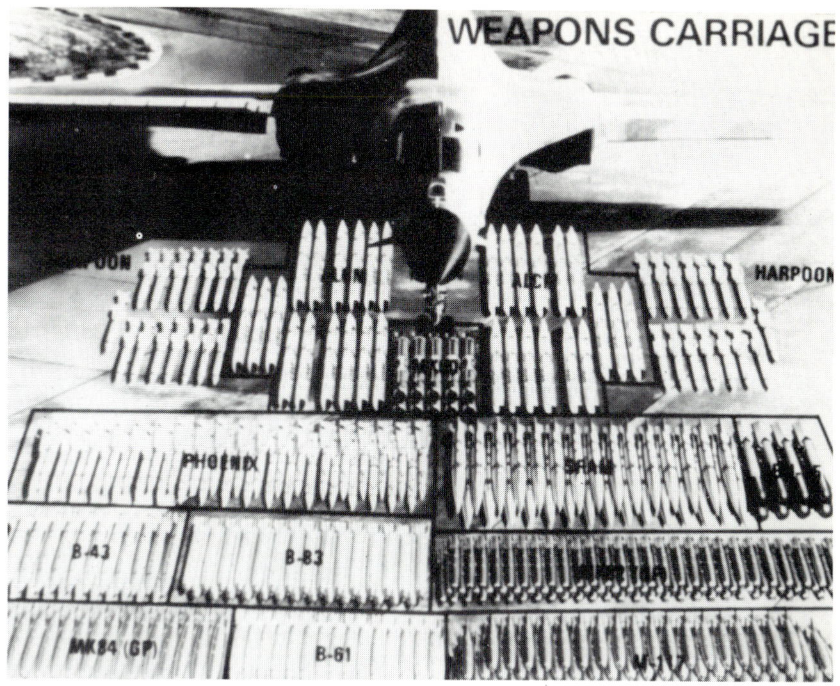

The usual PR photograph shows everything that will physically fit into the aircraft, whether it will become operational or not. At this writing, the only weapons that are certified for the B-1B are the B61, B83, and AGM-69 SRAM. Testing is continuing on conventional munitions.

At left is a left side view of the multipurpose launcher used in the B-1. It holds eight weapons, and rotates to release them at the six o'clock position. A right side view is seen in the photograph at right.

The MHU-196/M loader is seen here with a multipurpose launcher that has been loaded with SRAM training shapes.

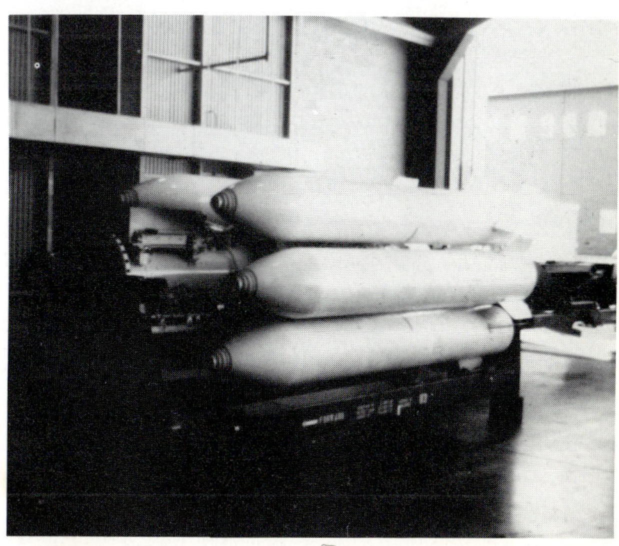

B83 training shapes (BDU-46/E) are loaded on this launcher.

Weapons bay fuel tanks hold over 19,000 pounds (3,000 gallons) of fuel, and are normally carried in bay one.

This multipurpose launcher is loaded with four B61 training shapes (BDU-36/E), and it is in place on the MHU-196/M loader.

The loading sequence begins with the MHU-196/M positioned under the weapons bay. Here the loader is starting to raise the launcher into position in bay two. (Zaloga)

The loader runs on its own hydraulic system which is powered by electric motors. It can place the launcher very precisely into position. (Zaloga)

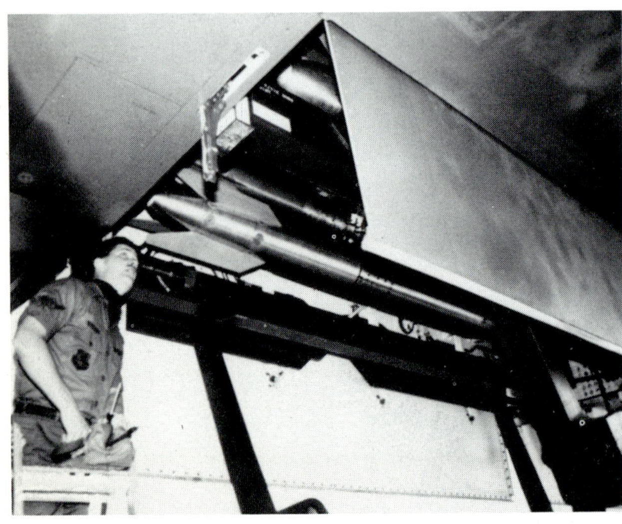

Above: At this point the launcher is nearly in position. Note the bay door safety handle. (Zaloga)

Right: This is the fully installed launcher with B61 shapes. The upper and lower racks do not have shapes loaded, because the sensitive clearance is on the sides. Therefore, the upper and lower weapons are not needed for practice. (Zaloga)

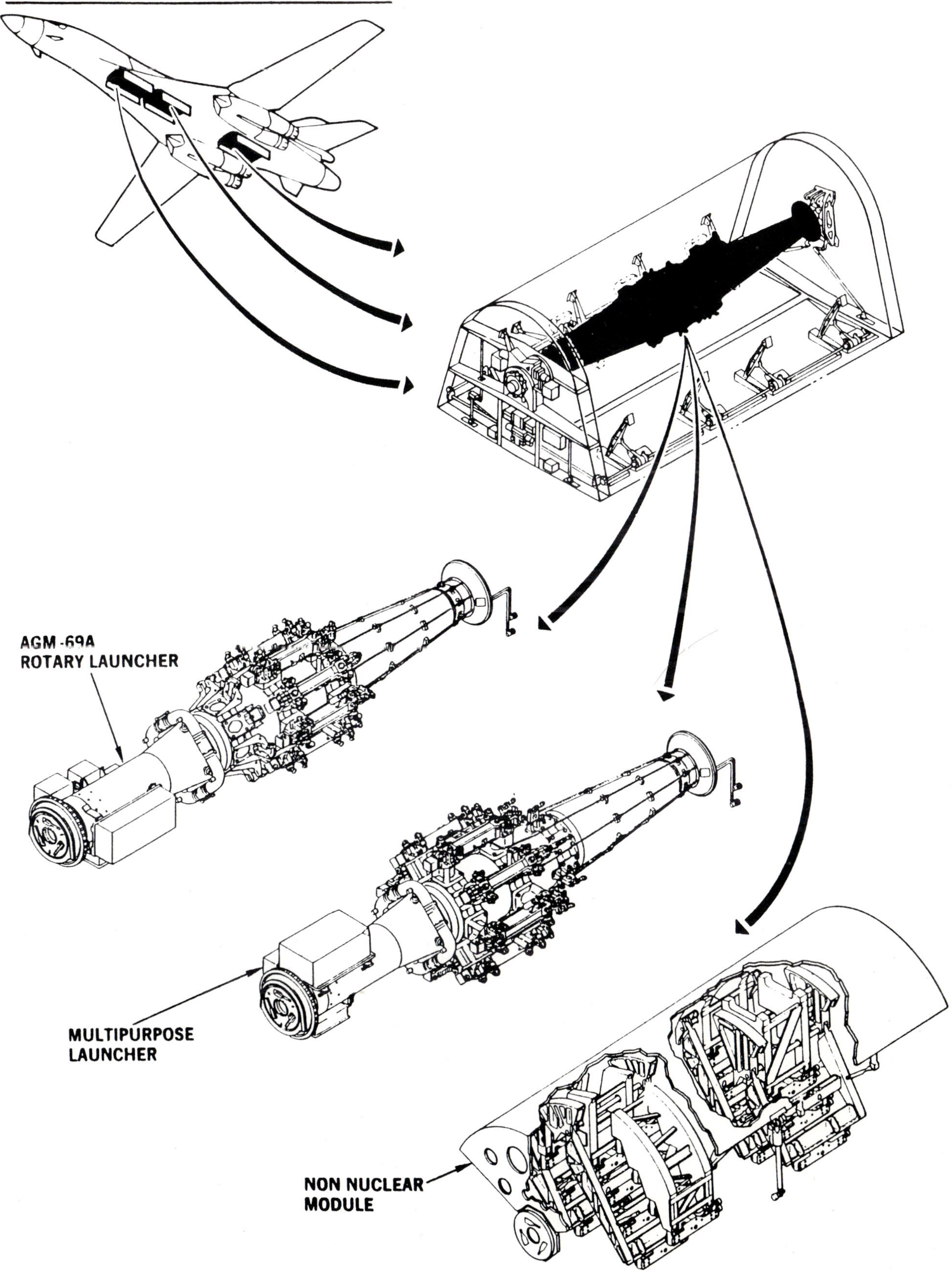

The multipurpose launcher is the only one currently in use with the B-1B fleet. The non-nuclear module is for "iron bombs," and drop testing is nearing completion.

(USAF)

red and blue trim. These are completely useless for an operational B-1B, and at present, there are no substitutes available. Hopefully, Monogram will reissue this kit with decals for an operational aircraft complete with nose art.

If you want to build a B-1B in 1/144th scale, this is the best kit to start with. Some corrections will have to be made, and the landing gear from an Entex or Minicraft kit could be used to build an "on the ground" model. It will take some effort, but a reasonable replica can be produced.

1/72nd SCALE KITS

Airfix B-1B, Kit Number 12003

This was one of the last kits released before the turbulence of financial problems overtook Airfix, and the kit obviously suffered. The decal sheet provides the tail number for B-1B number two, but the color scheme is based upon speculation that the production aircraft would be painted in light gray and slate gray finish. It never was! An instrument panel is on the decal sheet, although it is representative of the panel in one of the early -As. Its blue color leaves something to be desired. Also provided on the decal sheet is the only representation of the expendable countermeasures covers you will find from any kit manufacturer.

The plastic parts in the kit are just not very accurate. The basic shape of the fuselage fails to represent the heavily blended effect of the real thing, and the shape of the nose forward of the cockpit is slab-sided instead of having a circular cross section. The same problem is found with the tail cone, which has been squashed out of round to a noticeable degree. The shape of the bottom of the fuselage is incorrect, lacking the downward swelling of the undersurface of the wing glove. It is nearly flat instead. The shape of the fin cap is also incorrect, and the engine intake lips are wrong as well. An attempt to model the RCS vanes was made, but they too are inaccurate. The rear windows for the OSO and DSO are represented only as raised panel lines.

Other problems include the vanes for the Structural Mode Control System (the small canards on the nose) that are supposed to fit into recesses in the lower fuselage. The base of each vane that fits in the recess is too large, and should be flush. The complex overwing fairing that adjusts to seal the gap behind the wing as it moves is not represented on the model. Instead, the fuselage is faired smoothly down to the engine pods. The wheel wells are not deep enough, and have no detailing. However, the landing gear itself is nicely done, and accurately represents the real gear. The problem with the gear is in its construction. The main gear consists of two halves joined vertically, and this results in a seam line that is difficult to remove. The other difficulty is that the main gear fits slightly off vertical, and with a four-wheel bogie, it is almost impossible to have all four wheels sitting flat on the ground.

Overall, the kit is fairly simple, has minimum detailing, and few options. It does contain moving parts in the swing wing assembly and for the horizontal tail surfaces. All panel lines and control surfaces are identified with fine raised lines, and repositioning the control surfaces on the wings or the rudder would require major surgery.

Interior detail is minimal and consists of a cockpit floor, an instrument panel, a rear bulkhead, two seats, and two control sticks. The seats look more like easy chairs than ejection seats, and should be replaced with ones that are more realistic. No rear cockpit area is provided.

The basic design of the model includes two large pieces for the upper and lower fuselage. With a model this large, it works out well since the lower fuselage piece has the landing gear mounts, and the weight of the swing wings is supported by this one piece and then directly by the gear. This means that there is no seam to crack later at the top of the fuselage due to the weight of the wings. The two fuselage pieces do not align well however, particularly in the forward area near the cockpit. The upper piece was about 1/16th of an inch narrower than the lower section. This resulted in considerable filling and filing to end up with a clean smooth fuselage.

Assembly of the swing wings is complicated by the way they are joined together. A thin rod is attached to both of the wings when the upper and lower halves are

Ed Sveum built this B-1B using the Airfix/MPC kit. This kit has shape and dimension problems as well as numerous inaccuracies and omissions.   *(Kinzey)*

glued together. This rod assures that the wings move together and both are at the same angle of sweep. The problem is that all gluing, gap filling, and sanding must be done very carefully to avoid damaging this rod. This is a rather awkward task at best. Once the wings are completed, they fit on short mounting posts on the lower fuselage, and are held in place with caps that are glued on. When assembled, the posts and caps provide sufficient support for the wings, but the gluing must be done carefully to prevent the wings from becoming permanently attached to the posts.

Other construction difficulties involve the moving horizontal tail, the fit of the vertical tail, and assembly of the engine pods. The horizontal stabilators are not balanced at the mounting pivot, and tend to drop to a vertical position. The easiest solution is simply to glue the stabilators in place. After all, how necessary is it for these to move on a model? There is a major gap between the fuselage and vertical tail that requires filling and blending. The engine pods consist of upper and lower sections with five intake baffles that fit into recesses in the two halves. Getting all of these pieces aligned is very difficult.

The forward bomb bay is partially recessed, and the bottoms of a fuel tank and two Air Launched Cruise Missiles (ALCMS) on a rotary launcher are shown. A third ALCM is included in the kit, and can be attached to the launcher. But all of this is really bogus, and it is probably best to leave this bay closed. The rear bay does not open, and is shown only by raised panel lines.

Overall, this is not a very good kit. The Monogram 1/72nd scale kit is better, but it too has its problems.

Ed Sveum, who was formerly with the B-1B program, and who is a member of IPMS/Atlanta, contributed to this review.

MPC B-1B, Kit Number 1-4551

This kit is a U.S.-produced version of the Airfix kit, and all of the comments pertaining to that kit are also valid for this one.

Monogram B-1B, Kit Number 5605

The first release of a B-1B in 1/72nd scale by Monogram appeared in 1983. It was marked with the same ficticious overall white scheme with red and blue trim as used on Monogram's 1/144th scale snap-tite kit covered above. It has since been released with decals and instructions for painting it in the operational camouflage scheme used on B-1Bs today. The kit number for that release is 5606, and it is covered below. A complete review is provided for that release, and except for the different decals and box art, all comments pertaining to 5606 also apply to this release as well.

The Monogram 1/72nd scale kit has many errors, but is clearly better than the Airfix/MPC kits in this popular scale. This model was built and photographed by John Wahl.

(Wahl)

Monogram B-1B, Kit Number 5606

The same plastic found in 5605 is also in this issue that was released in 1986. This time the plastic is dark green instead of white, and the markings are for the "Star of Abilene" presentation aircraft. It is painted in the Strategic Scheme now on operational B-1Bs.

Measuring the model reveals that it scales out to 1/75th scale in length, and 1/74th scale in span. Therefore, the finished model will be a little undersized, but not so much as to be obvious. The molding is the usual crisp job that is expected from Monogram, but there are some big problems with the kit. There are no less than seventeen separate cruise missiles supplied, and there are mounting holes in the fuselage for them. This is totally inaccurate, since in actual practice there is an individual small pylon for each missile. The only B-1Bs equipped to carry them are the two test aircraft at Edwards Air Force Base. But unfortunately, that is the smaller of the problems. It appears that the original molds were based on a B-1A, then changed to the B-1B configuration later. This in itself would have been fine if the job had been done properly, but it was not.

Starting at the nose, the forward avionics bay ahead of the nose gear well is too short as the photographs and drawings in this book will show. The nose gear drag link is the long version fitted only to the first three B-1As, and the EVS, that was only fitted to B-1A prototypes, is also included. The vents on the bottom of the fuselage just forward of the weapons bay are for the prototypes only, and in the wrong location to boot. The same can be said of the small antennas that are also located there. The boundary layer exhausts for the B-1A's engine inlet system still remain, and the shape of the inlet, as viewed from the front, is pinched at the top instead of being rectangular. None of the intakes or exhausts that are located at various places in the skin of the B-1B are included, and the multitude of antennas on the real aircraft have been ignored.

The construction of the model is straight forward, and is easily followed on the excellent instruction sheet. The fuselage comes as upper and lower halves, and requires filling and sanding along its entire length to remove the seam that results from its assembly. But the fit is generally good, and the seams are easy to get to for the body work. However, this is the most time-consuming part of the construction. The seam between the clear cockpit/ windscreen part and the fuselage also requires filling and sanding.

The swing wing mechanism is adequate for support of the wings through the entire sweep from full forward to the fully swept position without any noticeable sagging. The cockpit is typical of that found on Monogram kits, and includes pilot and co-pilot figures. The crew access door can be positioned opened or closed as desired, and the boarding stairladder is provided. Missing are the windows for the OSO and DSO positions. Panel lines are raised on the fuselage and recessed on the wings. Landing gear and wells are nicely done.

The model shows the heavily blended surfaces of the aircraft, and can be made into a decent replica, but it will take much plastic surgery to do so. It might be easier to convert the kit back to a B-1A. However, if a 1/72nd B-1B is desired, this is still a better place to start than the Airfix/ MPC kit, simply because the shapes and dimensions are better.

Tom Starnes, a modeler and member of IPMS/Atlanta, contributed to this review.

1/48th SCALE KITS

Revell B-1B, Kit Number 4725

This is the first release of what has to be the best and most accurate model of the B-1B released in any scale. This initial issue has decals for several B-1As, and none for any B-1Bs, so they are unusable. This is because the kit accurately represents a B-1B, not any of the B-1As. The desert camouflage scheme, shown on the instruction sheet, was never carried by any B-1B. The comments provided below for kit 4900 apply to this issue as well with the exception of the decal sheet.

Revell B-1B, Kit Number 4900

Although it has a few flaws, this is the best kit on the market of a B-1B. If you simply want to build an accurate model of the B-1B, and don't care what scale it is in, and if you have a lot of room to display the model once you have finished, this is the kit to buy.

Among its shortcomings are the "one size fits all" panel lines. While they are of the more desirable recessed variety, they are all a uniform size which is overscale. There is no difference between the panel lines that represent the joining of panels that fit closely together and those that represent control surfaces such as flaps, slats, and spoilers.

The kit scales right on the mark for span, but comes out to about 1/50th scale in length. This translates to

This model was built by Tom Starnes of IPMS/Atlanta, using the Monogram kit. (Kinzey)

The large Revell B-1B in 1/48th scale builds up into a credible B-1B, and with some extra detail work, it can be turned into an outstanding model.

being about four scale feet short, and it is spread throughout its length. Therefore it will be impossible to accurately correct the problem. But this is the only kit to include a weapons bay load that is accurate, with SRAMs and a bay fuel tank being provided. The weapons bays themselves are well detailed with the multitude of cable runs on the aircraft being nicely represented.

The landing gear is the proper configuration and is well done. However, it would be wise to replace the plastic axles with metal ones, since the model is quite heavy when finished. There are some things that could have been done better by Revell, considering the scale involved. These include the navigation lights, which are only shown as engraved panel lines, and the many intakes, exhausts, and antennas that have been ignored. The model suffers from the lack of a good representation of the seals that close the gap aft of the wings when they are in the forward position, but this is the case on most models of aircraft that have wings of variable sweep. This problem is compounded on a model of this size. The simple solution is to build the model with the wings aft and leave them that way, but the better answer is to scratchbuild the seal and leave the wings forward. Built straight out of the box, the wings move, but are not interconnected.

The other big problem with the kit is caused by its sheer size. The fuselage is so wide in the center section that it needs some internal bracing and bulkheads, and even then a case of the sags may effect the wings. The fuselage is divided into the same three sections as the real thing-forward, center, and aft. Some work with filler and a file is required, since the fit between the sections is not all that it could be. Due to the size of the parts and the need for thicker plastic, the wings in the review kit were warped to the extent that only one of them could be saved. Revell provided a replacement for the other.

Most of the rest of the model is made up of various sub-assemblies that are excellent modeling projects in and of themselves. The complete cockpit assembly is highly detailed, although it is almost hidden inside the fuselage once the kit is completed. The nose gear alone has seventeen parts, and the main gear has forty-seven parts. The weapons bay and SRAMs comprise another ninety-eight parts. Decals are provided for B-1B number one in the initial factory roll-out scheme.

We recommend this model, but it will take a lot of time to do it well, partly to make corrections and improve the kit, and partly because of its sheer size and complexity.

DECAL SHEETS

To date, only one decal sheet has been issued for

models of the B-1. It is the Superscale (formerly Microscale) sheet 72-577 in 1/72nd scale. It provides markings for two aircraft. One of these is B-1B number twenty-five, 85-0065, based at Dyess Air Force Base, and the second is B-1B number thirty-five, based at Ellsworth Air Force Base. Some stenciling is also included.

The instruction sheet contains several errors, incorrectly locating the 28th Bomb Wing at Dyess AFB. As a former member of the 28th BW, I can assure you that it was, and still is based at Ellsworth AFB. The callouts for Federal Standard numbers and their locations on the drawings is incorrect, and includes FS 16473, which is the almost white underside color used on tankers. The national insignias are a light gray with clear areas for the background color to show through for the star and bars. They are close for the one on the bottom of the right wing, but incorrect for the aft fuselage. With that exception, the decals themselves are good. Just ignore the color scheme instructions and follow the drawings and photographs in this book.

Two other sheets, both issued first by Microscale, and now by Superscale, may prove helpful to modelers building kits of the B-1B. These are sheets 72-274 in 1/72nd scale, and 48-104 in 1/48th scale. Both of these decal sheets provide U.S. national insignias in low visibility subdued tones.

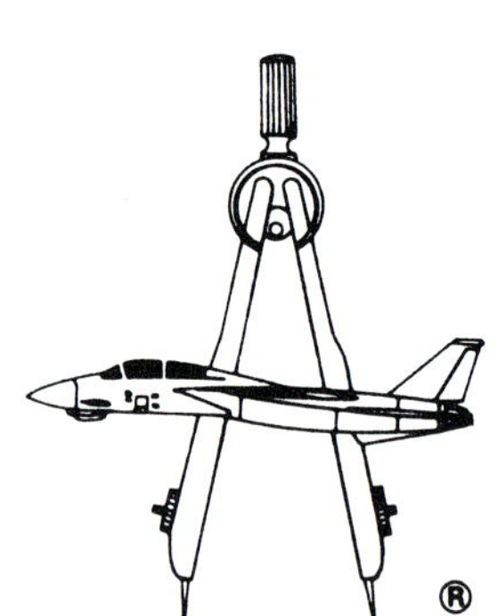